THE BANK OF ENGLAND BEDSIDE BOOK

in three volumes

Volume I

A Thread of Gold

Adventures, Escapades and Memories

Other compilations by Paul Tempest

Qatar 1967-2007: A Strong New Bridge

The Manila Surprise 1762-1764

The Old Lady Overseas

The Old Lady at Play

An Umbrella for the Old Lady

Re-Threading the Needle

The Bank of England Bedside Book

Volume I: A Thread of Gold
Adventures, Escapades and Memories

© Paul Tempest 2008
(All contributors retain individual copyright)

Stacey International
128 Kensington Church Street
London W8 4BH
Tel: +44 (0)20 7221 7166 Fax: +44 (0)20 7792 9288
E-mail: info@stacey-international.co.uk
www.stacey-international.co.uk

ISBN: 978-1-905299-89-8

CIP Data: A catalogue record for this book is available from the British Library

Compiled by Paul Tempest

Designed by Kitty Carruthers

Printed in Singapore by Tien Wah Press

THE BANK OF ENGLAND BEDSIDE BOOK

in three volumes

Volume I
A Thread of Gold
Adventures, Escapades and Memories

conceived and compiled by

Paul Tempest

being an assemblage of his and other contributions from
The Old Lady of Threadneedle Street (1921-2007),
The Threadneedle Club (founded 1985) and
The Threadneedle (founded 2008)

Drawings by Danny Denahy
Cartoons by Basil Hone

STACEY
INTERNATIONAL

'Now get out there and **WIN**'

CONTENTS

CONTRIBUTORS

Some Comments on this Book

"Sandwiched between a thoughtful introduction and conclusion, Paul Tempest has compiled a charming, affectionate and eminently readable *pot pourri* of offerings from the archives of the Bank of England over the three hundred and more years of its existence." – **Nigel Lawson**

(The Rt Hon Lord Lawson,
Chancellor of the Exchequer 1983-89)

"Here we have a combination of delightful sketches and thoughtful reflections which all add up to a valuable portrayal of the Bank of England – coming at a time when a better understanding of the Bank, and its central role in the financial and commercial integrity and success of the United Kingdom was never more necessary.

"Recent events have shown how unwise it was to diminish the powers and position of the Bank of England in City affairs. This book is a first balanced step towards re-thinking the regulatory hiving-off decision and making the UK's entire financial structure and operation once again 'as safe as the Bank of England'." – **David Howell**

(The Rt Hon Lord Howell, Secretary of State for Energy
1979-81, and for Transport 1981-83)

"Anyone who has worked in or alongside the Bank of England over the years will enjoy Paul Tempest's light-hearted collection of anecdotes and reminiscences about Bank people. What echoed for me were the names of so many of them I had been teamed up with from time to time in my Treasury days, in delegations to international bodies like the OECD Working Parties, the IMF/IBRD meetings, and in bilateral discussions with representatives of the US Treasury and Federal Reserve. Others I knew later from my spell of five years inside the Bank. It is good to be reminded by this book of how able and colourful so many of my Bank colleagues were." — **Douglas Croham** GCB

(The Rt Hon Lord Croham, formerly Sir Douglas Allen,
Permanent Secretary, HM Treasury, 1968-74, Head of the Home
Civil Service, 1974-77, Chairman, British National Oil Corporation
1982-85, Industrial Adviser to the Governor of the
Bank of England 1978-83)

"Paul Tempest began his career in the Bank of England managing the Reserve accounts of the State of Kuwait. Since then (1961) he has kept up an enduring friendship with my country leading to the year 2000 when, with the late Sir David Gore-Booth, we together founded the Windsor Energy Group as a new facility for briefing and consulting the Ambassadors in London and, where appropriate, their governments on energy and energy-related matters. This new book also expounds the value of long-standing trust and respect." — **Khaled Al-Duwaisan** GCVO

(HE the Ambassador of Kuwait to the Court of St James,
Chairman of the Arab Ambassadors in London, and
Dean of the Diplomatic Corps, London)

PREFACE

Bleak House

First impressions of the Bank of England have been, for the general public over the last 250 years, not at all good. Bleak, windowless walls stretching along Threadneedle Street and all other sides signal a fortress, secrecy, exclusivity, for some, a prison. Here are things that have to be hidden, people who have to be guarded, numbers not to be disclosed, papers not to be seen. The atmosphere pervades to this day.

The massive portals convey stuffiness and formality. The Messengers, some pink-clad, some drab, check the briefcases and handbags of visitors with appointments, turning all others away. The tourists in their open-topped buses and Londoners in their double-deckers stream by, seeing nothing. The outside walls, built after the Gordon Riots of 1780, are strong and thick and high, and are designed to keep the public out.

All the casual visitor might see, if venturing inside, is the Main Entrance Hall – a neo-Greco-Roman temple with lofty marble and basalt pillars and an amazingly delicate mosaic

'I used to think the Treasury was slow in taking decisions.'

1

flooring laid down by Boris Anrep in the 1930s, that has survived stiletto heels and for its first 40 years, the boots of the daily detachment of the Brigade of Guards. Beyond, perhaps a glimpse of the garden, where in 1922, they delayed the cutting-down of a century-old lime-tree until the fledglings born in the nest in its branches had flown off.

Hard Times

After a 50-year involvement with the Bank, my own emotions are somewhat different, a mixture of pride of having been so involved, affection for many good friends and colleagues, and respect for what the Bank has achieved over the past 314 years. It has, in my view, served its country and the national interest soundly with sustained serendipity and minimum fuss.

Latterly, however, particularly in the recent litigation regarding BCCI, the Bank of England has passed through some hard times, where its integrity and that of some of its staff was challenged. Throughout this long legal process, the Bank could not defend itself day-by-day against these allegations whether directly in public or through the media. As a result, some of the more virulent papers took the Bank's silence as an admission of guilt. Gradually, however, the inconsistencies of the charges became more and

'Of course, the big problem here is still recruitment.'

more apparent. Distrust was replaced largely by sympathy, understanding and affectionate support. Finally the litigants' case began to crumble under its own weight. After a final spirited and well-argued defence, the Bank of England was vindicated completely.

Great Expectations

The secret of the success of the Bank of England turns essentially on its ability to balance and reconcile the interests of the private-sector and the demands of government for financial order as well as for cash. Caught between the grasping hand of government and the seething turmoil of the market-place, it has to be vigilant and it has to be discreet. Above all, whatever it decides has to be within a range of acceptance by either side and to satisfy the legal framework and working practice of the day.

There is another prerequisite for the success of the Bank of England that is sometimes ignored or forgotten. It is the issue of the motivation of the people who work within its walls. They are neither driven by the expectation of high government office, nor are they promised huge material gain. They have to be prompted, indeed inspired, to work effectively and creatively together. They have to engender confidence and trust in all around them. And they have to be discreet.

In an age of automated on-line banking and multiple daily communication by e-mail and mobile involving billions of automatic responses from often remote computer centres, it is easy to lose sight of the fact that it is the people who matter, the individuals who make up the staff of any organisation.

The Old Curiosity Shop

This book does not aim to be an economic or historical treatise on the Bank of England. For this you must look first at the Official Histories or the many popular works on the subject. It aims to gather curiosities about the Bank, a collection of random insights, including my own, which together will, I hope, give a brief composite impression of the internal dynamism of the Bank.

One key to unlocking the secret of Bank of England morale and understanding the *esprit de corps* that lies behind its success has been the Bank of England's quarterly magazine, *The Old Lady of Threadneedle Street*, founded in March 1921, which expired at the end of 2007. Its origins lie in 'The Bulge', the flood of staff returning from the trenches after the First World War and having to settle back uncomfortably into daily commuting and their 40-year careers with the Bank. There were clearly far too many of them. They had seen many bad things. They were critical of the Bank's old-fashioned ways, restless for new opportunities. The new magazine, sponsored by the Governor, (later Lord) Montagu Norman, and heavily subsidised, set out to give them a voice, a controlled outlet for frustration and discontent, an opportunity to write and publish with strong links to the wider London literary scene. Above all it encouraged those who felt the need to explore new ideas and not to take themselves or their fellows or their masters too seriously. Something 'between *Punch* and *Private Eye*', with the Governor having the final word. Until a month before the publication of Issue No.1, it was to have been called *Wild Thyme*. Then the Governor intervened, remarking that he was not sure that working-time in the Bank of England of 1921 was quite as wild as all that.

As explained elsewhere, I was lucky to acquire early on from a Bank widow all the issues of *The Old Lady* back to March 1921, so that I now have the complete set of 346 issues. I quickly realised they held a treasure-trove of Bank stories as well as a host of eccentric and adventurous characters. These I began to set down in my *Wild Thyme* series of *Old Lady* articles covering life in the Bank with relevant anecdotes and character sketches. They, together with the more recent booklets of reminiscences compiled for the Threadneedle Club, form the framework of this book, the first of a series of three.

A Christmas Carol

Where does the Bank of England go from here? This I leave for the last chapter. For the time being, the Bank is in sound and responsible hands. Over the past ten years, the Bank of England has reinvented itself to meet new demands and new circumstances. Every aspect of its operations and administration have been placed under intense scrutiny and subjected to a thorough overhaul and upgrade. Together with a re-definition of its core purposes and a quantum leap in its intelligence-gathering, this represents an immense achievement in so short a time.

Since 2003, as explained in the Conclusions, a new strong foundation has also been laid for the Bank to play a much wider role in central bank and financial sector relations worldwide.

For the longer term, there will be new challenges , but also great opportunities. Staff motivation will be vital: shrinkage, currently 5 per cent p.a., has to be stabilised before it is too late. The Bank has to break further out of the mould if it is to survive and prosper.

In the world at large, confidence in the Bank of England remains unshaken. In a troubled and unstable world economy and increasingly globalised markets, the issues of business integrity, employee motivation and involvement are still relevant.

'My word is my bond'

'The lender of last resort'

'As safe as the Bank of England'

All these concepts have been widely known, admired and respected worldwide for over three centuries, a thread of gold through our history. We need to know that this precious thread will be there for our future.

A Very Old Lady

You're a very Old Lady, the young maid said,
    Just two hundred and twenty and eight.
Why, oh why, do you make such a terrible fuss
    When I'm only a tiny bit late?

In the days of my youth, the Old Lady replied,
    I was taught to begin work at nine,
And now that I am old and just rolling in gold,
    I still cut my breakfast quite fine.

You are now very old, yet all through the War
    You kept hours that were quite dissipated;
How did you get through all you managed to do,
    With energy still unabated?

In the days of my youth, the Old Lady replied,
    I never put work before pleasure,
I always attended the Derby and Oaks;
    For the *Times* I found plenty of leisure.

You are old, yet you frequently take on fresh jobs,
    From 'Currency Notes' to 'Conversions'.
Most folk of your age are inclined to bath-chairs,
    And gruel and such-like diversions.

In the days of my youth, the Old Lady replied,
    I had breakfasts of beef and champagne,
That greatly developed my biceps, of course,
    And also augmented my brain.

I've just answered three questions, and that is enough.
    Just get on with your work, you young person,
Or you'll very soon get three months' notice from me
    And your next job you'll find is a worse 'un.

A G Rowlett, 1922

CHAPTER ONE

Landmarks in the History of the Bank

1694 – 2008

Shorts from Reports

- Should be encouraged to go far (upwards unlikely)
- His ceiling is in the basement
- Should be as far-flung as the Empire used to be
- A real treasure – should be buried
- Wants understanding
- Worth his weight in dross
- Superficial from top to bottom
- Gives more trouble than he takes
- She has been tried but found wanton
- Goes without saying
- Makes everyone well when he goes sick
- Would poison a snake if bitten by one
- Wet with bright intervals
- Has apparently studied economics and the art of indolence
- Slow but unsure
- Under a rough exterior, he conceals an interior just as rough
- Uses a sledgehammer to crack nuts that aren't there
- Carries a lot of weight, but only below the collar
- Do not agree he should be shot; how about arsenic?
- Will do anything for anybody – right up to the hilt
- All he attempts becomes a tour de farce
- Has reached great heights – all he needs now is a little push
- Bellicose before lunch, comotose after

Extracts from Flyleaf *published in* The Old Lady 1932–2007

10

Landmarks in the History of the Bank

1694 – 2008

1694 Established by a charter of King William of Orange and Queen Mary, the Bank of England aimed to create a new central institution along the lines of the Amsterdam Wisselbank founded in 1609. It broadly satisfied threefold pressure for a new national bank:

- To raise large volumes of money for the UK Government on a continuous basis, most particularly to finance the British and Allied Army then fighting the French and Spanish in Flanders.

- To establish credit-based trading on a sound basis to expand London's role in international trade and to help develop rapidly the industry and infrastructure of the UK economy.

- To create an indissoluble link between the UK Government and the merchant community in the City of London.

William Patterson, a Scotsman resident in London, drafted the proposals reflecting the instructions of Charles Montagu, Chancellor of the Exchequer, for a 'Fund for Perpetual Interest' to which City merchants could subscribe with confidence. The first Governor was Sir John Houblon, a leading member of the French Huguenot refugee community in London.

The Bank opened for business in 1694 in the premises of the Mercers Hall in Cheapside, moving within a few months to the Grocers Hall in Poultry. The original staff of 19 included the chief cashier, the first 'accomptant' and a secretary/solicitor, each at £200 pa, 10 tellers at £50 pa and two doorkeepers at £25 pa. The first staff instructions prohibited business 'after candlelight' and required the Staff to be fenced in 'to keep people from disturbing them'. In the Grocers Hall, a Watch based on eight specially selected watchmen was set each night at 10.00 pm precisely. During the working day, the Gate Porter wore a gown of crimson cloth and carried a large bamboo cane, apparel still in use on important occasions today.

1745 The Jacobite Rebellion of 1745 prompted a heavy run on the Bank with large crowds of depositors demanding gold and coin for bills of exchange and notes issued by the Bank. It became clear that the Bank would need much larger reserves of gold and a more rigorous management of its liabilities if it was to survive further crises. Monetary stability became – and remains – the prime objective of Bank policy.

Since 1724, the Bank of England had pursued a policy of purchasing any property that became available in Threadneedle Street until a 25 metre frontage had been established. This continuing expansion swallowed up three taverns ('The Sun', the 'Fountain' and 'The Ship'), two coffee houses ('The Bank' and 'The Garter'), several shops and warehouses and the church of St Christopher-le-Stocks. By 1828, under the supervision of the Bank's architect (from 1788 to 1833), John Soane, the entire island site had been surrounded by a high, strong, windowless, stone-clad wall, as it is today.

1780 In the Gordon Riots of 1780, the Bank was twice attacked by the mob. A strong military force was sent to defend the Bank. After the rioting had been quelled, a military guard of 30 led by a subaltern officer and sergeant arrived each night to guard the Bank, and continued to do so each night until 1973, when their responsibilities passed to the Bank's own specialist security staff. The task of securing the Bank vaults and keys and keeping a close eye on the military fell each night to The Official-in-Charge, his Deputy and the Superintendent of the Watch, all drawn from a monthly rota of Bank officials, but their various duties were gradually slimmed down and, within another ten years, were transferred to the Security Staff Control Room.

1797 From 1793, the Napoleonic Wars placed acute financing strains on both the Government and the Bank. As gold reserves shrank and high inflation took hold in the economy, the Government reacted in 1797 by declaring the Bank's notes inconvertible, a restriction not lifted until 1821. The shortage of coin was met by the issue of Bank of England £1 and £2 notes.

1826 The County Bankers Act of 1826 permitted the Bank to establish branches in major provincial cities, strengthening the position of the Bank in economic surveillance and facilitating the distribution of Bank of England notes. By 1833, all the Bank's notes over £5 had been made legal tender.

1844 The Bank Charter Act of 1844 reserved the right of issue and replacement of notes to the Bank of England on condition that these Bank notes were backed by gold coin or bullion. A fixed price for standard gold was announced, ushering in a long period of price stability.

Fixed annual staff leave was introduced in 1845. Prior to that, the Staff enjoyed Bank holidays (47 working days in 1761 but these were gradually whittled down to 17 in 1830). Early closing on Saturdays was introduced in 1860 and lasted over a century until Saturday was abandoned as a working day. The Bank of England Staff Library was established in 1850, providing a handsome and comfortable reading room with a generous flow of new books and periodicals and a lecture programme. The subscription, covering the loan of two books at a time, was set at 10 shillings (50p) and remained at that level for over a century.

1890   When Baring Brothers, a prominent private merchant bank, gave clear signs of imminent bankruptcy, the Bank of England recognised the wider danger to the reputation of the City of London and stepped in. A guarantee fund of £17 mn, provided mainly by the leading stock banks, was established and the crisis averted. From then on, it was widely assumed that the Bank would intervene whenever there was a risk of collapse by a major city bank or other leading financial institution.

1914   The First World War (1914–1918) again placed enormous financial demands on the UK Government. The link with gold was broken and an attempt in 1925 to restore the gold standard quickly failed. A formal abandonment came in 1931 when the country's gold and foreign currency reserves were transferred to HM Treasury, although the day-to-day management of these assets remained and remains today with the Bank of England.

1920   In 1920 the Governorship of the Bank passed to Montagu Norman (1920–44). Under his direction, the entire island site behind the outside walls was excavated and rebuilt, destroying what Pevsner described as 'the finest collection of 18th/early 19th century buildings then remaining in England'. The seven above-ground floors and three vault floors of the new building provided ample modern, state-of-the-art facilities for the Bank staff which had expanded at the end of the First World War and which received another major boost in 1939 when the Bank took over the administration of UK Exchange Control (1939–1979).

In March, 1921, under the strong personal support of the Governor, who referred to it frequently as 'my passport round the world', the Bank of England's lavish quarterly magazine, *The Old Lady of Threadneedle Street*, was launched. It ceased publication in December 2007 and is being replaced by an annual magazine, the *Threadneedle*, produced by the Bank's alumni club, The Threadneedle Club.

1930 The establishment of the Bank for International Settlements (BIS) in Basle, Switzerland in 1930/31 coincided with the increasing involvement of the Bank in setting up new central banks and other currency authorities in Latin America, Eastern Europe, Africa, Asia and the Pacific areas, and also its underlying concern for efficient global financial consultation, co-ordination and, whenever necessary, action.

1946 The nationalisation of the Bank in 1946 made remarkably little impact on its operations and day-to-day management. It had long been moving away from purely commercial business to seeking to strengthen its various functions within the public sector. It nonetheless remained an active and vigorous player in the London financial markets and continued to fulfil the function of 'lender of last resort'. The economic strength of the UK had been sapped by the Second World War (1939–1945) and the Bank was faced with a succession of foreign exchange crises which greatly impeded the country's economic recovery. These culminated in the devaluation of sterling in 1967.

1968 A major obstacle for the UK economy at this time was the fact that the bulk of foreign exchange holdings in many countries were held in sterling. Through the Second World War and in the immediate post-war period they had been piling up and, as a multiple of UK gold and foreign exchange reserves, constituted a recurrent threat whenever the holders, anxious to invest in their own economies, sought to switch large volumes for US dollars or other hard currencies. The 1968 Sterling Agreements, negotiated by the Bank with over 40 major sterling-holding countries and backed by a massive international credit facility organised through the BIS, proved highly successful in stabilising sterling by providing a guarantee in US dollar terms.

1976 The high growth in money supply and accompanying fears of hyper-inflation prompted the Bank to introduce money-supply targets as a new instrument of monetary policy. They were reinforced in the early-eighties, but by then the impacts of revenue from UK oil and gas development in the North Sea were well on the way to underpinning the UK economy. 'Monetarism' as it was called, then entered a period of progressive discreditation and abandonment.

1997 In 1997 the in-coming Labour Government took the decision to transfer working responsibility for monetary policy and the setting of interest-rates to the new, independent, Monetary Policy Committee in the Bank of England. Its instructions were to set and manage interest rates in such a way to achieve the Government's target for low inflation. Debt management on behalf of the Government was transferred to HM Treasury and the Bank's regulatory functions were transferred to the new Financial Services Authority (the FSA).

2008   The Bank of England defines its two core purposes as:

1.   *Monetary Stability*
Monetary stability means stable prices and confidence in the currency. Stable prices are defined by the Government's inflation target, which the Bank seeks to meet through the decisions on interest rates taken by the Monetary Policy Committee and their subsequent transparent and efficient implementation in the money markets.

2.   *Financial Stability*
Financial stability entails detecting and reducing threats to the financial system as a whole. Such threats are detected through the Bank's surveillance and market intelligence functions. The risks of such threats are reduced or eliminated by strengthening the infrastructure, and by financial and other operations, at home and abroad, including, in exceptional circumstances, by acting as the lender of last resort.

The lender of last resort.

CHAPTER TWO

Esprit de Corps –
Proud to be There

The Clerk's Lament 1830

On 5 August 1830 the Court of Directors of the Governors and Company of the Bank of England gave formal notice that henceforth only 17 specified working days would be observed as Holidays at the Bank, prompting the wide circulation of The Clerks Lament penned by Mr Burrowes of the Power of Attorney Office beginning:

And have you heard the doleful news,
Alas, and is it true?
If all the Holidays are gone
What are we Clerks to do?

In vain the Steamers daily ply
To waft us with delight
To Margate, or to Ramsgate pier
And back again at night.

We kept the days of all the saints
Right primitive were we;
And now have we renounced them all
Like heathens as we be.

We once kept hold of Lord Mayor's Day,
And also Powder plot –
The Parliament may now blow up
And we care not a jot.

A Cornerstone of Life

Peter J Bull

A penny for a spool of thread
A penny for a needle
That's the way the money goes
Pop goes the weasel

Friendship can be a cornerstone of one's life. The old Bank – that is before I retired from it over twenty years ago – was conducive to the development of friendships in a way that I think might be less so in the present Bank. That might be a consequence of the change in attitudes to work and leisure, and to the opportunities available in a more money-driven society, but the Bank, I would like to think, still generates a special atmosphere in which relationships, working and leisure, flourish.

Six Months Counting Coin

Joining the Bank in my teens as an 'uncovenanted clerk' (whoever could have dreamt up that title?) and being consigned to the Sub-Vault for six months to sort coin (something that also befell Leslie O'Brien some forty years before he became Governor) introduced one into an atmosphere where one's relationship with one's colleagues was not so very different from that at the school one had just left. The working day was nine to four, and the forming of friendships was a natural consequence of the situation one found oneself in, growing partly out of a feeling of solidarity in a shared experience that was hardly what one had expected on being employed by the Bank of England but to which it would have been unforgivable to indicate any objection.

Those were the halcyon days. One could have a quick lunch for a shilling and then go to Alfred Hayes in Cornhill to try out the latest recording on 78s of a Mozart or Beethoven symphony, and still be back at one's coin counting machine within the hour. And in my case it was a mutual love of music (and later of cross country running) rather than the shared experience of sorting or sifting coins in the Sub-Vault that help cement a friendship that lasted nearly sixty years and was for long the key antidote to the Bank and desk work.

The Bank of those days seemed positively to encourage leisure activities in a way that I am not sure that it does now. I do not think it encouraged the clubs and societies simply because it realised that working for the Bank could often be boring and frustrating. Nor do I think it did so because it wanted its employees to feel more friendly disposed towards it than it knew many to be. I think the upper echelons actually believed it was a good thing to do.

Developing Relationships after Dark

In those days the Operatic and Dramatic Society was in its heyday, and helped lots of young men and women forget the Bank and discover soul-mates. And so did the Sports Club, although there were still separate Men's and Women's Clubs and some of the sporting relationships were more developed after dark. The Library and Literary Association was a different matter because in the 'Clerks Library' one was not allowed to utter a word; the atmosphere could be frightening! But all the clubs and societies helped the staff to get to know one another and that was conducive to close attachments and marriage, as well as to life long friendships.

The Bank's staff then totalled around six thousand, and however many people asserted that they hated the place, the routine nature of much of the work could be relieved by coffee, lunch and tea breaks in Tokenhouse Yard or its equivalent, which enabled people to escape to friends and fellow spirits and talk about things that did matter, and this was also conducive to the establishment of more than just 'good working relationships'. Thus, for many in the Bank, friends – not the work – became the dominant element in their lives. This was not enough to stop some people 'quitting' (to use the Bank's preferred term) because of frustration, non-fulfilment, disappointment at realising that one's qualities or abilities were not fully appreciated or sometimes the stuffiness of the working environment. But for lots of reasons, of which perhaps friends and the social side were the major one, many remained 'loyal'.

A Wonderful Place to Get Away From

With the contraction in the Bank's work which started in the 1970's there began a much bigger outflow into other City jobs and sometimes elsewhere, and many found they were better at doing their new work than they ever thought they could have been. They discovered they had qualities and the capability to excel far beyond what had seemed required in the Bank, and some really shone. Some even discovered that the Bank had taught them something without their being aware of it. They could stay members of their Bank clubs and societies and retain their friends still in the Bank, and be more fulfilled and happy. Why should those relationships change because of a change in employment?

In those days one could still enter the Bank to see one's friends. In my younger days one could even walk into the Bank and unchallenged go down the spiral staircase to the Sub-Vault and see gold ingots being wheeled around. That of course had to change but even when I retired it was not like visiting a prison, as it is today. In correspondence one is still dealt with in amicable terms but there is hardly a welcome for the visitor. But it is still nice to be greeted by a pink-coated gentleman on entering the Front Hall, even if the security man has to treat you as a potential terrorist.

Change is Inevitable

When one reaches the stage where the number of people working in the Bank that one actually knows can be counted on two hands, does that really change one's perception of the place? We see an institution that still happily employs some non-graduates, though it may be more difficult for them to move up the ladder, and despite academic qualifications some of the rest do participate actively in the clubs and societies, and the Bank seems

more integrated as a whole than it used to be. Its reputation
for professionalism seems undiminished even if on menial
matters one may think that standards have dropped. I am
sure that no one is now sacked if for a second time they
make a mistake that gets out of the Bank. No one is sent
home for wearing yellow socks. No woman clerk is given a
warning never again to wear culottes in the Bank (or, dare
I mention it, for not wearing another item of clothing).
The pensioner, however, may have to be careful not to
raise an eyebrow at the sight of a male employee with an
earring or two, or something similar on a nostril. And away
from the work many sports and social activities still
flourish, meaning that many individuals still very much
enjoy the company and friendship of their colleagues away
from the Bank.

The UK has undergone astronomic change over the
past sixty years. Inevitably the Bank is now a totally
different place having been transformed from what was
needed in the poverty stricken post-Second World War
years to what has been required for adaptation to the
European Union and an integrated world monetary system.

The Threadneedle Club – A Measure of Diversity

Thousands have left the Bank and taken jobs in other
financial institutions or further afield. You just have to look
at the membership of the Threadneedle Club to see the
diversity of their jobs. One may well ask why so many wish
to gather together regularly for a convivial dinner or
reception. The main reason is, I think, to meet again old
friends and sparring partners but beneath the surface is a
sense of still enjoying some ties with the great institution,
The Old Lady, and having worked for it during an
extraordinary phase of its existence. What a privilege!

And time moves on leaving eventually only the best
memories.

Peter J Bull joined the Bank of England in 1945, aged 16. In the Overseas Department, he was for four years the Alternative UK Executive Director (1972–76) to the IMF, Washington DC. He retired in 1985 as Deputy Head of Banking Supervision.

He was also Chairman of the Bank of England Sports Club (1969–72 and 1977–84).

After retirement from the Bank, he became Executive Director of the UK affiliate of Société Générale (1992–97) and was also Honorary Treasurer of the Royal Philharmonic Society (1991–2005).

Proud to be There?

Leslie K O'Brien

*I*n my experience, most of those who spend any considerable number of years in the Bank's service leave it with regret and recall with pleasure the years they have spent there.

I realise that the thoughts of one who entered the Bank not so long after the end of the first world war and only a little before the world was plunged into a depression which lasted until the second world war may bear a stamp which separates him from his younger colleagues.

Are colleagues proud to be in the Bank?
Do they regard themselves as members of an élite?
Does loyalty to the Bank and concern for its good name come
before personal interest?

I hope so but I am not so sure as I was forty years ago that the answer to all these questions is an unhesitating affirmative. The world has changed and like so many older men I do not like all the changes I see.

Some changes in my lifetime have been very much for the better. Greater equality I count the best. The end of discipline imposed without reason or explanation is good too and so, of course, is the higher general level of prosperity which helps to give those who share it confidence and a proper pride in themselves. Servility has always been unattractive and its disappearance is one great improvement in our age.

As is usual, gains are not made without losses. Mindless loyalty and unquestioning obedience are better dead, certainly, but does it make us all happier to throw out the baby with the bathwater? Fewer and fewer of us nowadays are ready to submit to the will of God, as interpreted by ourselves or by those who believe themselves to be in His confidence. Are we prepared to submit to anyone's will but our own and is this the recipe for continuous happiness? I doubt it.

It has become fashionable today to talk about the under-privileged at a time when the description is less justified than ever before. In my day, those who came from poor homes, as I did, really were under-privileged, but the thought that they were simply never occurred to us. Life was there to be lived. We did not feel sorry for ourselves and would have resented the impertinence of anyone who presumed to be sorry for us. I wish there were more of that spirit today. Perhaps among those concerned there is and it is merely the politicians and the press who are hypnotised with their own catchwords. I hope this is so.

Leslie O'Brien is the only person in the 314-year history of the Bank to enter from school aged 19 and to leave as Governor (1966–73). It took him almost 30 years from entry in 1922 to reach Deputy Chief Cashier (1951–55). By way of contrast, Eddie George, the only other home-grown Governor, entered as a graduate in 1962 and took half the time, a mere 15 years, to reach the post of Deputy Chief Cashier. Both took the same length of time – another 15-16 years – to progress from that appointment to that of Governor.

Leslie O'Brien had enquired when he was 18 about entry into the Bank but had been told that a Director's nomination was essential. He knew no one remotely close to the Court of Directors, but, by chance, spotted in the newspaper that Lord Revelstoke had just been appointed a Director. He wrote immediately, congratulating him on his appointment and pointing out that, as indicated by his address at the head of the letter, he lived in a very modest house in a very modest street named Revelstoke Road, London SW and would therefore be most grateful for his Lordship's nomination. It arrived by post a few days later.

Also essential for entry into the Bank in 1922 was a pass in the handwriting examination conducted by the London Chamber of Commerce and acceptable marks in the Bank's own entry examinations. When, aged 84, Lord O'Brien addressed the Threadneedle Club Annual Dinner in 1987, he was introduced by (Sir) George Blunden brandishing a standard Bank of England staff file marked prominently LK O'BRIEN and purporting to be the entry examination papers completed by Leslie in 1922.

Only in the Bank of England (and very few other institutions worldwide) would no one question that a Deputy Governor could just pop down into the Sub-Vault and collect the full set of papers and marks of an examination conducted 64 years previously.

In his inimitable schoolmasterly way, George held up the file and said how disappointed he was with what he had found. There was a pause before he continued.

Leslie, who for 50 years in the Bank had always been held up as the model of the Clerk Who Could Do No Wrong, looked genuinely perplexed, having clearly no idea what was coming.

'Handwriting – 60 per cent,' announced George with a shrug of the shoulders.

'Arithmetic – 65 per cent.' Another pause. 'English Essay – 50%.' Another shake of the head.

Leslie looked horrified, as if some ancient secret – unknown to him – had just been revealed.

'However,' George went on sweetly, 'He has done much better since.'

Leslie rose to speak, pulling himself together and bravely squaring his shoulders. Sitting between the two of them, I was able to catch Leslie's arm and pass him a note saying, 'He's just joking, you know!' Leslie smiled, relaxed and delivered his 25 minutes on 50 years in the Bank of England. It was, as always, packed with wit, wisdom and common sense. He was rewarded with a well-deserved and affectionate standing ovation.

CHAPTER THREE

The Eye of the Needle

(Chief Cashier's Office 1809 – 1989)

Experto Grede – CCO, 1922

As I went out for my glass of stout
    At noon the other day
I met in the Yard a curious card
    Who seemed in a hopeless way.

And as I paused to see what caused
    His dismal and sorry plight,
He started talking, and with me walking
    Gripping my forearm tight ...

'You see, I'm lent, for experiment,
    To the CCO, pro tem:
But they want men so in the Tellers, you know,
    I'm actually working for them...

'I was sent for last year by the Chief Cashier,
    And given to understand
That with my brains, if I took pains,
    My prospects were simply grand.

'I thought it a bore in the Cashier's store
    (Though not really as bad as it seems)
I swallowed my bile, and said with a smile
    It's the Office of my d--- reams.'

The Old Lady, June 1922

The Eye of the Needle
(Chief Cashier's Office 1809-1989)

In 1989, the Chief Cashier's Office, or CCO as it was known, ceased to exist as an independent office in the Bank after a life of 180 Years. For generations, it had been the eye of the needle through which all juniors had to pass to have much hope of rapid promotion in the Bank. Here Malcolm Gill, who was Chief Cashier through the period of closure, explains why, Guy de Moubray gives some impressions and Mike Clancy describes how antiquated the procedures had remained in 1986 when he was one of the last to complete the weekly Bank Return by hand.

Miss Words and Mr Figures

'I knew her well, Miss Words'

The three golden words in bold capitals above the CCO entrance portals on the ground floor draw the eye upwards. At seven each evening, one guardsman of the Nightly Watch on duty there kept sentry while the daily business and accounts of the Bank (and the nation) were completed and balanced in manuscript each night by the lone 'waiter'.

Inside the Chief Cashier's Office, the eye was again drawn upwards to the top of the two massive pillars where presided, on each side, elderly Mr Figures and his CCO paramour, Miss Words. What message is to be drawn from these two enshrined permanently by the Bank in stone, Mr Figures, a wizened older man with a goatee beard, moustache and wild hair composed of the numerals 1-9 and various mathematical signs presides over a hand-operated adding machine with side-lever and a roll of paper, a lecherous old devil if I ever saw one. And also in her proper place at the top of her own pillar, the delectable Miss Words, her long hair composed entirely of letters of the alphabet to match the letters on the keyboard of her manual typewriter. I knew her well, Miss Words. What is clear is that, according to the Bank of England, Words and Figures, like men and women, are fundamentally different, and will remain so, yet should always, in surroundings such as the Bank, try rapidly to reach agreement.

For the numerate (and all budding Chief Cashiers were alleged to be able to cast with 100% accuracy thirty entries of 16-digit sterling balances within sixty seconds in their head – including the shillings at 20 to the pound, pennies at 12 to a shilling and farthings at 4 to the penny) CCO held no fears. For such as I – with little more than basic military training with the infantry, an explosives certificate from the Royal School of Military Engineering and a smattering of medieval French and German – it was a source of astonishment that we had been allowed to blunder into such a shrine for arithmetical maniacs and that, far from being offered up as a temple sacrifice, we had been recalled to endure further months of indoctrination, trial and torture. It was only when we were despatched abroad alone to run a central bank of our own, that we began to understand the point.

Gone by then was all the verbal finesse and cerebral speculation about monetary theory and economic modelling. All you needed to run a central bank anywhere in the world was an unshakable conviction that the way the Chief Cashier's Office of the Bank of England did things was right and that anything else was probably wrong. We had been hired by people and governments who believed, rightly or wrongly, in the absolute standards of the Old Lady. If anyone of importance questioned that standard or failed to endorse our decisions. we were simply to show them our return air-ticket to London and announce our departure. If we hesitated, we would be lost. Thus, similarly, the Brigade of Guards and the Royal Navy, of which the Bank overseas was little more than an imperial extension, a thin red line which few monetary infidels dared to cross.

Two weekly tests of stamina barred the way of every CCO entrant. Mike Clancy describes below the rigours of the Bank Return suffered alone often deep into the night, but, first, the weekly Tender by the market for Treasury Bills for the following week.

Here was what has been described as a mixture of the *Inferno* and the *Mikado* enacted weekly from 1.00 to 1.30 pm on Fridays, a perverse *Alice in Wonderland* Court of Justice with the Queen of Hearts and full retinue intent on decapitating any playing-card servant who stepped out of line.

The Tender was determined in the theatrical surroundings of the octagonal Committee Room adjoining the Court Room. Beneath its 18th Century Venetian chandelier and deep in its richly patterned custom-made Wilton carpet, the room was laid out in my time with five tables, two seats behind each., representing the five working days of the following week, in a half-circle facing the table for the senior officials. No calculators, mechanical or electrical, were allowed; no computers, no slide rules. With the ten clerks assembled, the huge pile of folded tender applications just received over the CCO Public Counter, would be sorted into the five days under the watchful eye of the Chief Cashier and a senior representative of HM Treasury with guest appearances from the Governors and Directors. On each table there would be a frantic sorting and totting up of the application forms at each price offered. The centre-table cross-checked that all was in order and proceeded to calculate the average tender price for the week. If there was a hitch, it was painful. Everyone, including the Chief Cashier, risked missing his lunch.

'Stand up, Monday!' announced the Chief Cashier in exasperation on one occasion after the two culprits had been identified. They left immediately for a sudden, unexpected new start in their professional lives elsewhere.

The Clapham Junction Role

Malcolm Gill

In its heyday – whenever that was – or, at least, when I joined the Bank, CCO was regarded as a sort of internal assault course (we now have Assessment Centres) which any aspiring clerk needed to complete if he (and it was he in those days) had ambitions to move up the Bank. The philosophy seemed to be that by moving people around rapidly and not allowing them to become experts at any job, one could test their ability to pick up a job quickly and do it well. As most of the jobs were related to the work of the 'Chiefs' of the Department, working in CCO was supposed to provide an opportunity for those Chiefs to make a first-hand assessment of the individuals working in the Office – and, less officially, vice versa.

CCO was also a great leveller. A young Third Class Clerk might find himself on the bottom end of the Central Banks Section ruling lines in 'rough books' in company with an Assistant from the distant Overseas and Foreign Office on the third floor who had already made his mark there and been sent to CCO on the basis that, if he could surmount the hurdle, wider opportunities in the Bank would become open to him. Certainly one advantage of this Clapham Junction role which CCO performed was that those working in it got to know their contemporaries and that the shared misery of CCO helped relationships with colleagues in one's later Bank career.

But times change. As the Bank began to need different skills and more specialists, the importance of mastering CCO-type work declined; and changes in work processes meant that jobs previously done in the Office either disappeared or could be done more appropriately elsewhere in the Department. As the Office shrank, we came to the conclusion that the balance of advantage in terms of management, staffing and cost lay in redistributing its functions elsewhere in the Department…

An Insistent Visitor

Guy de Moubray

A number of amusing incidents happened at the CCO Counter to which the public were admitted. I once went to the counter when an extraordinary looking woman with an ashen face appeared.

'I have come,' she said, 'to collect a million pounds which King Leopold of the Belgians has deposited here for me'.

'Yes, madam,' I replied, 'I'll make enquiries, may I have your name.'

'Mata Hari,' she replied.

I went back to my desk, looked at a few papers and returned to the counter to tell her that there was no record of any such deposit and suggested that she should go and see the Belgian Embassy.

City of Human Memories, *from which this extract has been taken was published in 2005. Guy devotes 160 of the 430 pages to a most* entertaining, frank and packed-with-anecdote account of the period of his Bank of England service (1950–76) including his impressions of CCO, his many trips to Basle and elsewhere and his secondment to the IMF in Washington DC. There are thumbnail sketches of almost all key players in the Bank and many others in or close to the Bank and a critique of how the Bank handled the issues in which he was involved. The index lists about 700 names including his direct ancestor, Roger de Moubray who crossed the Channel with William the Conqueror, fought at the Battle of Hastings and was created Earl of Northumberland, and grandson, Arthur de Moubray born in Caen in 2002 and, according to the records, the first in the direct line to be born in Normandy in over 900 years.

The Bank Return Handwritten

Mike Clancy

In the summer of 1986, I compiled 11 weekly Bank Returns during my three months on Books Post in the Chief Cashier's Office. I still have copies of 'my' Bank Returns as a memento of the oddest job I ever did in the Bank.

First of all, there were the hours. Every day you started at 7.30 to 8.00 am. On Mondays and Tuesdays, you went home at about 1.00 pm and on Fridays at about 11.00 am. Wednesdays and Thursdays were a different matter. On Wednesday evening you compiled the Bank Return, no matter how long it took. In my case, I remember getting away as early as 10.00 pm, but I also remember two occasions of not escaping until almost 2.00 am. On Thursday, after say, three to six hours' sleep, and having first prepared the weekly figures for Court, and then ensuring the Bank Return was published at 3.00 pm, you settled down to do the 'mish-mash' (the seven-week forecast of the money market position), leaving at about

8.00 pm – so another working day of 12 hours or more…

A colleague at the time suggested that the unchanging mystique of CCO was a deliberate attempt to prove the reverse of the US Navy system. It was said that the organisation of the US Navy was designed by geniuses to be run by idiots, whereas the CCO system was designed by idiots to be run by geniuses.

In 1931 the Maharajah of Rewa visited CCO and subsequently presented the office with a large revolutionary machine some four feet by two feet which accurately multiplied and divided quite large sums to the astonishment of all. It was placed reverently on display at the back of the office, being deemed to be of no practical value to CCO.

'We can't quite decide whether to make you an Advanced Trainee or offer you an early pension.'

CHAPTER FOUR

Kenneth Grahame &
The Wind in the Willows
1908

Messing About in Boats

There is nothing – absolutely nothing – half so much worth doing as simply messing about in boats.

The Poetry of Motor Cars

The poetry of motion! The real way to travel! The only way to travel! Here today – in next week tomorrow! Villages skipped, towns and cities jumped – always somebody else's horizon.

Both from The Wind in the Willows *by Kenneth Grahame,* 1908

Badger, Toad, Ratty – which one are you?

A hundred years on, every line still resonates. All human life is here, all politics, all hope and dread...

Politicians are easy to spot. Tony Blair may have fooled us into thinking he was a competent, companionable Ratty, with his gleaming coat and twinkling eyes, but we should have identified him much sooner as Toad.

Ah, Badger! Who can fail to identify that dour, gruff, morally upright, unsociable creature in his prudently-dug earth? 'Badger, hates Society, and invitations, and dinner, and all that sort of thing.'

Was there ever a better, briefer summary of instinctive xenophobia?... That suspicion of the Wide World endures; Ratty and Mole are the fretful British electorate in times of globalisation, no doubt about it. There is also a worried underclass of rabbits and squirrels, 'a mixed lot' whose main aim is not to lose their homes or to be mugged by stoats.

Libby Purves, *The Times* 20 May 2008

Kenneth Grahame & The Wind in the Willows

2008 – A centenary

Kenneth Grahame is, by far, the most prominent and popular literary figure to emerge from the Bank of England. Yet there remains a great mystery about him, about the circumstances of his departure from the Bank and about his subsequent rather distanced relations with the Bank.

In 1908, he tendered his resignation to the Bank Governors on the grounds of fearing a mental breakdown due to persistent ill-health and increasing pressure at work. His masterpiece, *The Wind in the Willows* was published later in the same year. Clearly there was a very strong link between the endearing children's story of the River Bank, of Mr Toad and Ratty and Badger and Mole, and the reasons for his abrupt departure.

As one of the top three officials of the Bank, he had held the post of Secretary, responsible for the administration of the Bank, with distinction for ten years. They were to be followed by 24 years more or less as a recluse in full retirement at home close to his beloved Thames.

What pressures clouded his last few years in the Bank and what prompted him to find an expression for his irritation and frustration? What other pressures were bearing down on him at this time? Literary scholars and critics have discovered some clues in his private papers and letters, but, as to be expected, the Bank of England has remained resolutely silent to this day. In this they have, of course, acted correctly but also, I presume, because successive Governors have found no merit in the image of a club of small animals and amphibians, albeit of a conservative disposition and comfortable lifestyle, threatened by a tumultuous, hungry and aggressive populace of stoats and weasels in the world outside.

A Difficult Childhood

To understand Kenneth Grahame and the strange world of *The Wind in the Willows*, it is necessary to know something of his early years.

He was born in Edinburgh in 1859. His mother died when he was five and he was sent to live with his grandmother and later with his uncle in Berkshire, close to the Thames. He last saw his father at age eight and at nine he was sent off to St Edward's School at Oxford. Bookish and described at the time as a rather lonely figure, he nonetheless won several school prizes and was made Head of the Sixth. Both at school and at home, as he later recalled, he found escape and comfort in reading and jotting down his thoughts, most often in summer on the river bank.

The young Kenneth had been greatly attracted to the idea of studying at Oxford and was looking forward to this. It came as a great disappointment to be told by his uncle that the family could not afford to give him a university education and that he was to earn his living in the City. A Director's nomination for entry into the Bank of England was secured through a family friend and he was duly despatched to the Bank to complete the entry examinations, including a handwriting test, a paper on arithmetic, and an essay.

A Mark of 100 Per Cent

Kenneth had no difficulty in passing these simple tests. For his English essay, he was awarded full marks, a mark which does not appear to have been matched in the Bank of England before or since. Not only did this success give him a special status in putting him on a track to rapid promotion, but it clearly fired his own literary ambitions. Reviews and articles appeared under his name and he was quickly drawn into the circle of Arthur Quiller-Couch, London journalist until 1892, critic, novelist and poet better known under his pen-name Q.

> *'Life's a jungle, life's a dance,*
> *See the mummers everywhere*
> *Hopping, tossing balls in air –*
> *How the hobby-horses prance!*
> * I advance*
> *Somewhat sick the round to share'*

Kenneth Grahame, from a poem published in the
National Observer, 1891

Grahame's book of essays and sketches, *The Golden Age*, was published in 1895 and its sequel *Dream Days* in 1898. They highlighted the gap between adults and children, the adults indifferent and completely out of touch with the real experiences of children – their frustration, their own griefs, anxieties and their anger at being so little understood. This struck an immediate chord with the critics and the reading public and both books quickly became best-sellers in the United States as well as in the United Kingdom.

Rapid Promotion

In the Bank of England, outside literary fame helped direct Kenneth's career towards the function of Deputy Secretary to the Court of Directors.

The Secretary's department was responsible for the minuting and organisation of its weekly meetings and, more importantly, for the administration of the Bank. The Old Lady was at that time entering a period of restructuring and modernisation and there were many pressing staff issues. From the post of Deputy Secretary, he was appointed Secretary in 1898 at the age of 38, one of the youngest in the 314-year history of the Bank to hold this position. He was remembered by colleagues as a rather aloof, taciturn figure but one who clearly held the trust and support of the Governors and Court of Directors. Even in March 1907, he was awarded a special bonus of £200, a clear indication of the esteem in which he was held.

Marriage and Early Family Life

While on holiday in Fowey with his friend Q (Arthur Quiller-Couch, later Sir Arthur and first King Edward VII Professor of English Literature at Cambridge), he met a young admirer, Elspeth Thomson and succumbed to her attentions and flattery. They were married in 1899 and one child, Alastair was born in 1900, blind in one eye and with a pronounced squint in the other.

Marriage seems to have come as a shock to Kenneth, aged 40. There were strains between Kenneth's habitual bachelor withdrawal into his books and solitary escaping to the river and Elspeth's demands for parties, dinners and the coming and going of friends and neighbours. Also Alastair needed close attention and Kenneth was away early each working day faced with a long commute by train to and from the City or isolated in a *pied-a-terre* in the West End.

In July 1903 Kenneth delivered an article to the *Chronicle* of his old school, St Edward's, quoting Caxton's *Golden Legend* about the boyhood of St Edmund of Abingdon. 'Hail, fellow, that goest alone', he writes:

'Not one-fiftieth the part of all your happy imaginings, will you ever, later, recapture, note down, reduce to dull, inadequate words,

but meantime the mind has stretched itself and had its holiday. But this emancipation is only attained in solitude... if there is another fellow present, your mind has to trot between shafts...

'... for company too often means compromise, discretion, the choice of the sweetly reasonable. It is difficult to be mad in company; yet but a touch of lunacy in action will open magic doors to rare and unforgettable experiences. But all these are only the by-products of walking alone. The high converse, the high adventures, will be in the country of the mind.'

St Edward's School Chronicle, Volume 12. No.321

A Turning Point

A turning-point appears to have come on 24th November 1903 when a visitor to the Bank during working hours suddenly entered his room, pulled out a revolver and fired three shots. Although uninjured, Kenneth was badly shaken by this episode and his health, aggravated by an operation and pneumonia, deteriorated. His work in the Bank was also affected by the prolonged absences of his Deputy on the grounds of ill-health. There were new responsibilities including the purchase and equipping of the new Bank of England Sports Ground at Roehampton (*see* Chapter 8) and from 1905 the Presidency of the time-consuming Bank of England Library and Literary Association, the BELLA (*see* Chapter 10). He was bullied unmercifully by one of the Directors and a change of Governors brought more strain.. His whole career, health and routine slowly began to unravel and by early-May 1908, he had taken the decision to resign.

In his resignation letter of 15th June 1908, he pleaded:

'constant strain in a post of much responsibility makes me very anxious as to my ability to continue rendering proper and efficient service and as to the wisdom of facing further deterioration of brain and nerve'.

Whatever strains there had been in the relationship, the Governors were most reluctant to release Kenneth Grahame. They offered a long holiday (up to one year) and read him the report of the Bank Doctor who had found no loss of memory or mental impairment. But Kenneth Grahame's mind was made up. He produced an independent medical opinion which diagnosed arteriosclerosis with symptoms of insomnia, constant headache, amnesia, depression and nervous breakdown. Reluctantly, the Governors agreed to an immediate retirement on half-pension. On 2 July 1908, while not yet 50 and after 30 years in the service of the Bank, he politely said his good-byes and left.

The Wind in the Willows Stories

Meanwhile, at home, there was further strain. Elspeth cared for Alastair, but found his facial expressions and squint an irritating embarrassment on social occasions. Kenneth loved the boy dearly and greatly enjoyed telling him bedtime stories and writing simple letters to him. The first references to these stories and an outline of the various plots and characters come from letters to friends and to Alastair. The first mention of Rat and Mole and also, incongruously, a Giraffe comes in a letter dated May 1904. A reference to *The Tale of Mr Toad* appears a month later.

The Wind in the Willows was rejected several times before being finally published in 1908 after Kenneth Grahame had left the Bank. There was scant acclaim for the first edition from the critics. *The Times* noted, for example:

'As a contribution to natural history, the work is negligible'

Gradually, after the inclusion of illustrations, the hostility and indifference of the critics began to thaw, triggered by some favourable reviews in the United States. Several prominent literary friends in London published eulogies and sales of subsequent and more child-friendly editions began an upward trajectory which reached 80,000 in one year.

The Reticence of the Bank

The *Wind's* popularity took the Bank by surprise. Montagu (later Lord) Norman, who had taken over the Presidency of BELLA (the Bank of England Library and Literary Association, founded 1850, see page 149) from Kenneth Grahame in 1908, was appointed Governor in 1920 beginning a term of office which lasted 24 years. One of his first acts was to create a new Bank of England Quarterly Magazine, *The Old Lady of Threadneedle Street* which first appeared in March 1921. It had high literary aspirations (see Chapter 11). Here, however was a dilemma. The greatest literary figure associated with the Bank, and then at the height of his popularity, was alive and well enjoying what turned out to be a 24-year retirement and basking in his acclaimed popularity.

So far as I can tell, there is no reference to Kenneth Grahame or *The Wind in the Willows* in *The Old Lady* until the year of his death in 1932. Even then there is no standard obituary as would be due to any senior official of Kenneth Grahame's rank and standing, chronicling his career and achievements. The September 1932 issue of *The Old Lady* carries a short note on Kenneth Grahame's literary works by a former colleague. There is no mention of what had happened to Kenneth Grahame in his 24 years of retirement. Or of the way Kenneth cared for Alastair during the first 12 years of his retirement and no mention of the apparent suicide of Alastair in 1920, knocked down and killed by a steam locomotive at Oxford. There are no condolences, no funeral or memorial reported, merely a drawing of him sent in by Elspeth Grahame. A terse, strangely worded announcement begins:

Mr Kenneth Grahame

Pensioners who live many years after their retirement from the Bank, and who seldom visit the scene of their former activities are apt to be forgotten except by the few with whom they were intimate, but the passing of Mr Kenneth Grahame concerns not only those who knew him as a Bank Official but all who have loved and read his books.

So for eleven years prior to his death, Kenneth Grahame had been able to enjoy reading, but had not been able to contribute to the sumptuous quarterly issues of *The Old Lady*, the perpetuation of a long literary tradition in which, inadvertently, he had become the jewel, albeit it appears unwelcome, in the Bank's literary crown.

Some Tentative Thoughts

What can we make of the Bank's actions and responses? What was being hidden and why? Locked in the Bank of England Information Centre and Archives are some of the answers.

Here are some of the points which strike me particularly regarding Kenneth Grahame and *The Wind in the Willows:*

The Political Dimension

We tend to think of the Edwardian era as an age of pre-World War One elegance and confidence. In fact the Government was often in turmoil. Germany's rising industrial strength was a challenge to the British Empire, reflected in the pre-World War One Anglo-German arms race and intense rivalry in establishing new African colonies. 1908 was the year of the launch of *HMS Dreadnought*, a new kind of battleship which transformed naval warfare. In the same year Baden Powell published *Scouting for Boys* preparing young boys for the rigours of military service, and of immense value in the trench warfare of 1914-18. Within Britain, the emergence of an extreme left wing threatened to undermine the state by revolution. Venerable national institutions such as the Bank of England were under no illusions about the danger. They could be expected to react with silence and caution to anything of a seditious nature. Firmly within this definition would be an account by a former employee of vicious class warfare translated into the adventures of several small furry animals led by a despicable toad resisting armies of stoats and weasels on and around a river bank.

The Stigma of Lunacy

Quite apart from the obligation of an employer to refrain from disclosing the medical details of any employee, the Bank would have been fully aware of the stigma attached to mental illness and the suffering caused at that time by the process of certifying insanity and committal to a lunatic asylum.

Kenneth Grahame had himself pleaded prior to retirement that he stood on the brink of nervous breakdown. Indeed, his assailant in 1903 had been arrested and promptly committed to be held on indefinite term in Broadmoor Prison. In order to protect Grahame and his family from prying eyes, given the high public interest in his writings, the Bank could be seen to be merely acting correctly as a shield for one of their more vulnerable pensioners and former top-officials.

Kenneth Grahame's Own Sensitivity

However disgruntled Kenneth Grahame might have been in the four years before his retirement, he did nothing in the next 24 years to promote his own cause at the expense of the Bank, remaining discreet throughout. He resisted suggestions by his publishers and others to publish his own memoirs or indeed to give any account of his time in the Bank.

The Death of Alistair

Another factor would have prompted Governor Norman

and the Bank to keep some distance from the Grahame family. To Kenneth's delight, he was able to realise his own frustrated boyhood dream of going up to Oxford, when he successfully enrolled his only child at Christ Church. Yet for Alistair, plagued by poor sight and disfigurement, this presented a great strain and bouts of depression.

One night, aged 19, he left college after dinner and walked across the town to a level-crossing on the edge of Port Meadow where he was struck by a steam train and killed instantly. But the police report which is still available notes that the body had not been found on or close to the level crossing, but several hundred yards up the track. There was no sign of the corpse being dragged there by the locomotive and there was no sign of a struggle or violence. The head had been severed cleanly and lay close to the rails. Kenneth Grahame and the college authorities were promptly alerted and were quickly on the scene. A verdict of misadventure was recorded by the Coroner.

In summary, therefore, both the Bank of England and Kenneth Grahame seem to have behaved correctly in making no attempt to publicise the circumstances of his retirement and in resisting those who wished to pry further into the personalities and opinions of those involved.

Who was Mr Toad of Toad Hall?

The man who caused Kenneth Grahame considerable anxiety and grief in his last years in the Bank appears to have been Walther (later Lord) Cunliffe, a Director appointed in 1895 and widely feared for his bad temper and maltreatment of the senior staff. There are contemporary accounts of a bruising confrontation between Cunliffe and Grahame which ended with Grahame's remark: 'You are no gentleman, sir.'

Cunliffe was a very strong character, but widely disliked both within and outside the Bank. Nonetheless, he was appointed Deputy Governor in 1911 and Governor in 1913, holding that position through the First World War during which he had a succession of angry exchanges and stand-offs with the Chancellor of the Exchequer, David Lloyd George. His nickname in the popular press was 'The Tyrant of the City'.

It is not difficult to spot the similarities of Cunliffe's appearance and behaviour and the mannerisms and attitudes of Mr Toad.

The other strong personality with whom Kenneth Grahame came into conflict was the new Governor appointed in 1907, William Middleton Campbell. One of the duties of the Secretary was to act as Private Secretary and Adviser to the Governor. For the first time, Grahame was faced with a Governor who was critical of his performance and reluctant to take his advice. In the same year, 1907, Grahame again poured out his anxieties in fiction. The short-story, *Bertie's Escapade* with its repeated theme of rejection and imminent redundancy, carried the leitmotif: 'Turn him out! Turn him out!'

Postscript

Even in the three-volume official history of the Bank of England 1891-1944 by Professor RS Sayers, first published in 1976, there is only one brief reference to Kenneth Grahame, and that is couched in distinctly unfriendly language:

> *'Even in the more responsible posts a man of intellectual capacity often found his mind only half-employed: Kenneth Grahame, for example, was able to write* The Wind in the Willows *and other books while he rose to be, and was for ten years, Secretary of the Bank. There were many others who were quietly exercising imagination and talents which were varied but found no expression in the art of central banking.'*

'The Deputy stepped over and looked me over, up and down. Before I could speak, he had seized hold of my umbrella, loosely furled, opened it carefully, shaken it violently and indicating severe disapproval, whirled it around his head a couple of times, causing a healthy *cordon sanitaire* to open up around us. The crowd, waiting for departure announcements, and energised by this performance like magnetised iron filings swinging into line, kept their distance, but watched closely, as if expecting a rabbit to pop out or the umbrella to disappear.

I stood rooted to the spot. Slowly, with infinite patience and practiced skill, the Deputy smoothed out each fold and rolling evenly, reduced my aged brolly to the diameter and appearance of Prospero's black staff. He handed it back without a word.'

From *Wild Thyme:* Carrying the Bag, March 1963, published in *The Old Lady*, September 1989

CHAPTER FIVE

Carrying the Bag

Standards of Dress

The signors of Establishments have issued a decree
Bidding sumptuary dissidents to conform and bow the knee.

So they dare impugn our judgement, they presume to doubt
our taste?
Tis shame the Bank's enlightenment at once should be
defaced!

Our dress must be more business-like (which business isn't
shown);
How I like it is my business; will they please to mind their
own?...

We must shun extremes of fashion; good idea, but not so
simple:
If observed, would we have ever dropped the crinoline and
wimple?

Why insult the female average of Bank intelligence?
Castigate the rare exceptions; leave the rest to common
sense.

from *Standards of Dress* by Parthenia, 1976

Carrying the Bag

The Overseas Department had other needles, other ways of assessing promising newcomers. Among these, the practice of the Governor taking a young member of staff with him to the monthly meetings of the Bank for International Settlements in Basle had its origins in the thirties, became regular practice in the fifties, sixties and seventies and still happens occasionaly today. In its heyday, nine or ten junior members of staff got a chance each year to travel with the Bank party and to be treated as one of the team. There was always the delight of first-class travel, some gourmet dining, occasional excursions and entertainments and an opportunity to see the BIS and the Bank team at work. All of this was good for morale. And the families remembered the Basle *leckerli*, Swiss chocolates, packet *fondu* and cuckoo clocks they were given on father's return.

There are many accounts of the monthly trips to Basle in *The Old Lady* going right back to the original establishment of the BIS in 1930. In 2005 there was another crop of these accounts by David Fecci, Roger Barnes and John Bartlett. Earlier contributors on the subject in articles, letters, obituaries and retirement notices include Anthony Williams, George Preston and Jane Mayhew. These cover the exploits and adventures of, among others, Lord Norman, Sir Otto Niemeyer; Lord O'Brien, Rupert Raw, Roy Bridge and Lord Richardson, including swimming the Rhine, climbing the Mont Blanc massif glaciers and finding one Governor in an ornamental pond draped in waterlilies.

The First Lady Bag-Carrier

After the practice was approaching the 30-year mark (and the total about 200 male carriers), it was decided, in the spirit of the age, to try sending a lady to perform the task. All went very well. The first *Koffertägerin* was young, with a merry Welsh wit and considerable Polish. A keen linguistic and musical ear and sharp eye made her a good listener and accurate observer. She also has an unfailing knack of reducing pointless theory, cliché and any hint of male prejudice to sound common sense and basic human values. In the essentially inward-looking planetary system of the Bank, she shone like a distant mega-star and was welcomed as such. Judith Smith insists most firmly, however, that on no occasion did she permit the Governor to carry her luggage.

This is Austria, Sir!

The most widely known story of the Basle bag-carriers was told to everyone who followed Scott. It formed part of the official briefing before any departure and, although it may have been embroidered here and there, it was nonetheless intended as a salutary lesson in not what to do but what not to do.

Scott – let us say, as I have no idea what the real name was – would have had a story to tell, that would have thrilled the heart of every Bank of England official, man or (later) woman – the stuff of dreams, if not central bankers' nightmares.

The Station Master at Liverpool Street Station had waved goodbye, as was his wont in full gold braid and top-hat. The Thursday afternoon crossing from Harwich to the Hook had been calm, uneventful and convivial. At the Hook, there had been some commotion – the cancellation of some other international express, but as usual, the Bank party had been whisked through the customs and crowded platform to their reserved first-class sleepers at the back of the Lorelei Express.

That evening, the whole party had enjoyed an excellent *coq au vin* and *crêpe suzette* in the panelled elegance of the Wagons-Lit Restaurant Car, washed down with half-a-case of Gewurztraminer, Sir Otto's favourite and always carried on board specially for him.

The whole party had retired to bed after much good talk and laughter. Scott, however, was still wide awake. The excitement of the trip, the excellence of the dinner and after-dinner stories had left him restless. For exercise, he took a long walk to the front of the train. There, every seat was taken and the corridors were crowded.

One traveller, clearly alone and sitting on a suitcase in the corridor, caught Scott's eye immediately. She was about nineteen, slim with long blonde hair, a fresh rosy complexion and a most disarming smile.

Flushed and excited, Scott recalled his instructions. No way could this be an attractive foreign spy planted to compromise the Old Lady and the British Government. She looked bored and tired. He decided to assault at once, meeting little resistance. Isolde was only too happy to talk. She was returning to Vienna, she explained in good English, after a year as an *au pair* in the Cotswolds. They chatted about the excitements and *ennuis* of life in London and Vienna. In accordance with his instructions, Scott did not, of course, divulge to a stranger, his destination or the nature of his own mission.

The train thundered on through the night, stopping

only once for about ten minutes. Reluctantly, Scott finally decided he had better get some sleep before morning and a busy day ahead. After exchanging addresses and making a decent goodbye, venturing a chaste peck on the cheek, he made his way back down the crowded corridor.

At the end of the corridor, he found that the connecting door to the next carriage was locked. Puzzled, Scott pulled down the window of one of the outside doors and looked back. He found himself staring, to his astonishment, back down the empty mainline, the rails shining hard, flat and silver and merging into a single ribbon in the clear, cold moonlight. The whole insubstantial pageant of the Governor, Sir Otto and four Bank of England Directors, together with all their luggage and the rest of the train, had vanished, melted into thin air, leaving not a rack behind.

Instinctively, Scott patted his breast pocket. There safe and sound, were his passport and ticket. There also, in his pocket, strictly in accordance with the Bank's instructions, were those of the Governor, Sir Otto and the rest of the Bank party together with all their Swiss Francs and other foreign currency.

Some hours later, just before dawn, some two-hundred miles to the West of Scott, an elderly male clad only in his pyjamas and occupying a first-class sleeper, was trying to explain himself to two highly suspicious German frontier guards. Like the bleary, sleezy, unshaven gang of elderly accomplices in the adjoining compartments, he possessed neither passport nor visa nor ticket. One of his friends was claiming to be *Banknotenpresident of the Konglichen Vereinigkeit*, whatever that was, yet neither he nor the bunch of tramps with him appeared to have a bean, let alone a note between them. For the ever-vigilant frontier guards, this merited further investigation.

Meanwhile, Scott's part of the train had thundered on relentlessly towards Vienna. The German-Austria frontier police removed him from it when they discovered that the strange, wild young *Engländer* was travelling with a large sum of money, no baggage and with passports and tickets under seven different names, one of which was a member of the House of Lords, three were Knights of the Realm and one had a German name. Again, further investigation was clearly required. Scott's lack of German did not help. Isolde, the only person who might have helped, turned away from the window in horror, as he was dragged down the platform gesticulating towards her.

Scott arrived back in Basle Hauptbahnhof on the Monday evening just in time to see the Governor's train to Calais pulling out, like Swiss clockwork, dead on time, with the Governor aboard. The Governor, at least, was back on schedule.

Swimming the Rhine

My account of how the late Rupert Raw was said to have swum across the Rhine at Basle during one of the monthly weekend meetings of the Bank for International Settlements was published in *The Old Lady* in September 1989. It was soundly based on gossip from the Parlours and the Nightly Watch which reported that, after the traditional Bank group dinner on the Saturday night, Rupert had so underestimated the strength of the river current that he had passed the Swiss-German frontier before he could find a convenient place to climb out and was thus obliged to present himself in the early hours to the German and Swiss frontier police and customs authorities without documents or belongings and, apart from a pair of sodden underpants, without any clothes.

The article immediately prompted two eyewitnesses to pen letters to *The Old Lady* each correcting a number of small details. Yet the accounts of George Preston and Tony (AJT) Williams differed markedly from each other and neither fitted two other accounts of the event, one published by Rupert Raw's journalist son and another in *The Old Lady* by Jasper Rootham and one by Sir Kit McMahon in *The Old Lady at Play* on the 'roasting' Rupert received the following day from the Governor.

Whether the swim took place early or late in the day or in the afternoon or after a champagne dinner remained in dispute. Tony Williams, a former Secretary of the Bank of England and thus an adept pourer of oil on troubled waters, offered the only plausible explanation: Rupert must have made a number of such swims, Basle being a hot and humid place in mid-summer and Rupert being Rupert

All I can add to this is my experience of working for Rupert for three years in the sixties when he was Overseas Adviser to the Governors. He was not only an extraordinary lateral thinker, but also often refreshingly eccentric. As a member of the Special Operations Executive, he had had an exciting War and Mrs Raw asked us on one occasion whether he was doing well in the Bank as he had never been quite the same after parachuting into Yugoslavia to join the partisans and landing on his head. He was highly regarded both by the Governors and all those who worked for him.

One of Rupert's eccentricities was his habit of starting the day by distributing the contents of his In-Box in small piles around the carpet. It was not unusual, on being summoned to his room, to find it apparently empty. A scuffling or rustling of paper would reveal Rupert's head emerging round a corner of the desk at waste-paper-bin level. On several occasions, I was cordially invited to join him on the floor, crawling around looking for whatever was lost.

Rupert Raw's Christmas parties in Chelsea and summer parties in Alresford for the European Group in Overseas were highly enjoyable and sometimes especially memorable as on one occasion when he had forgotten he had invited us and failed to tell anyone at home. We were welcomed warmly by Mrs Raw with a cheerful equanimity that signalled that this was not the first time it had happened. The party was already in full swing when Rupert arrived home, and, with a look of bemused astonishment, enquired what the reason was for such a surprise.

Talking Turkey

Roger Barnes

We were always told that the founding fathers of the BIS chose Basle for their new institution because it was the best rail hub in Europe in those days before civil aviation (and because there was a five-star hotel going begging near that railway station to use as an HQ).

The most regular attendee from the Bank at the pre-war meetings was Sir Otto Niemeyer and he used the train service to travel – even during the 1950's when flying became a serious option (a central banking Dennis Bergkamp). His usual route was via Dover, Calais and Paris on the Silver Arrow service, but reasonably frequently, as a change, he used the Harwich, Hook of Holland down the Rhine route on the Rheingold Express.

Lord Cromer usually went to Basle by aeroplane, but for the month I was selected as bag carrier he decided to try the Rheingold Express route. This created something of a panic in Secretary's Office because the route was at least five years old and a lot of rusty levers had to be pulled.

I was hauled down for a briefing and handed a small leatherette notebook with comprehensive manuscript instructions for the bag-carrier. It rapidly became clear that both the rail routes involved an orgy of tipping – and the bag-carrier was given very precise instructions as to when, whom and with how much to tip…

At Harwich the book said that we would be met by the stationmaster, the duty harbourmaster and the ship's Purser. Problems loomed when we assembled an escort of only two: a short man with a rather scruffy off-white braided cap and a taller, non-uniformed man in a duffle coat. I team up with the cap and hoped to play it by ear. The cap made to peel off as we left the railway station, so I reached into my silver pocket and proffered two half-crown coins. He gazed at them ruefully. 'Not like the days of Sir Otto Niemeyer, sir!'

After we had ushered the Governor into his cabin I turned to the duffle-coat. I was at this stage seriously underspent on the UK leg so I decided to make up ground and offered him two pounds ten shillings. He was seriously offended: it emerged that not only was he a director of the shipping line but a distant relation of the Governor to boot. I went to my own cabin in somewhat chastened mood.

As a wry postscript, a few years later, when I was private secretary to the next Governor, we were asked to review the list of gifts that were sent out at Christmas in various directions, on the Governor's behalf. This was in the course of a major economy drive following the report into the Bank's internal administration by McKinsey, the management consultants.

It emerged that each year since at least 1950, we had been sending a turkey to the stationmasters and harbourmasters at Dover and Harwich. In the circumstances, we did not feel that an annual saving of four turkeys would seriously discommode the Governor's travelling style, so the axe fell.

Sterling Devaluation
David Fecci

December 1967

Supper over, two of the party walked home through the snow along the banks of the Rhine, while the less energetic piled into a taxi. Back at the Schweitzerhof, past midnight and with 18-hour fatigue fast setting in, I was hailed in the foyer by Mr Roy Bridge:

'Not off to bed yet, are you?' Come and have a drink.' And for the next two hours in the hotel's bar I listened spellbound as the Guardian-in-Chief of the pound sterling, defeated (he felt) but certainly unbowed by recent events, unwound by relating the story of the devaluation. The story, gripping enough in its own right, was further enlivened by snarling commentaries on the spinelessness of politicians. My kingdom for a pocket tape-recorder!

'Taking the global view is all very well, but we also like you to be able to do the work.'

Shopping for Sugar

John Bartlett

I went in 1973. Most bag carriers were working in the Overseas Department, which is where I had been since starting in the Bank some three years beforehand. I was a last-minute substitute, the rumour being that the original choice had become so nervous at the prospect that he had retired to his bed with a diplomatic illness. And indeed the stories around the department painted a daunting picture of bag carriers facing a host of challenges in a strange country, using an unfamiliar language and with senior Bank staff treating you as the lowest sort of minion.

But it wasn't like that at all, though I can see that it might have suited some returning bag-carriers to give the impression that it was...

The visit was otherwise uneventful, until Governor Richardson took me aside and said that he had something that he very much wanted me to do. Nerves started to kick in as I wondered what it was that others in the building were better equipped to supply.

'My wife and I would be so grateful,' he said, 'if you could possibly go out into the town and buy some sugar for me to take home.' For some reason that I now forget, there was an acute sugar shortage in the UK at that time, and I think that my most important contribution to the weekend was to help relieve it for the Governor.

'The answer is No. What was the question?'

'A perfect example of unnecessary duplication.'

CHAPTER SIX

The Overseas Office

The Overseas Office

The gutting of much of the East side of the Bank in the devastating fire of 25 September 1986 finally extinguished the last traces of that remarkable cockpit of fledgling central bankers, that 'haunt of gifted amateurs', that 'casino of dreams and nemesis', the old Overseas and Foreign Office – not only responsible for dealing with people overseas such as our friends in Australia and Fiji, but – when necessary – with foreigners such as those to be seen at Boulogne or Calais.

Governor Montagu (later Lord) Norman set up the new office in 1932. His instructions were: 'to be knowledgeable about everything that might affect British trade or the position of sterling'

As British trade was worldwide and sterling was used to settle most of it, this was quite a formidable remit. Within a very short time, however, the Government – and particularly the Treasury, the Cabinet Office and the Foreign Office – expected the Bank to provide instantaneous comment, detailed briefing and answers to parliamentary questions on almost any economy in the world and to give considered guidance on where the UK national interest lay.

Some of the members of Overseas seemed to rise like the phoenix from the ashes of their past with the Chief Accountant or the Chief Cashier. Some dropped like stones through the murky waters of international finance. Others appeared from nowhere and vanished abruptly. Many happily pursued with passion their particular area of responsibility while apparently completely oblivious of the often highly confidential, if not secret, tumult of activity going on around them. Yet all those I knew who had been caught up in that curious, remote, imperial time-warp looked back with warmth at the friendships and loyalties ignited so spontaneously within it.

The office was located on the Bartholomew Lane (East) side of the Bank on the third floor. It was a long, low, side-lit room. In the early-Sixties when I joined it from the Chief Cashier's Office, the room had very much the character of a cow-byre. The bulky four-man desks (barely a single woman then) – two clerks to each side – were placed regularly end-on between the side-walls and a long central strip of carpet, down which the messengers would march briskly at intervals tossing work and requested files into the wooden Group In-Boxes on either side, like so much fodder for the day. In my time one messenger was given a generous efficiency award for suggesting that a single flat piece of wood of a length one inch greater than the length of the In-Box and of a width one-inch less would, when placed in an empty In-Box, provide a gradient such that incoming work , piled above about six inches, would slide off onto the floor and thus demand attention. Otherwise it was a quiet room, untroubled by typewriter or calculating machine, where the telephones were picked up on the first ring and voices were usually subdued.

'Next time you talk to Berlin,' I was advised by the Chief Clerk after trying to make myself heard on a bad line, 'try using the telephone!'

In the stalls between the desks, the rustle, rumble and swish of purposeful literary digestion – shared sixty-fold – was broken only by the occasional thud of a dictionary closing or belch of a card-index.

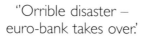

"Orrible disaster – euro-bank takes over.'

A History Little Known

Peter Edgley

I was lucky enough to serve in the Overseas Department from 1956 till I retired – almost thirty years, or half the independent life of the office. For someone with a life-long interest in foreign countries and the diversity of the human race, it was a great place to be.

In the 1950s, London was still the hub of a great empire. The colonies and dominions, plus a few others, formed the Sterling Area, using London as the 'bank' for their exchange transactions. Their main trading partner was the UK. Indeed, half the world's trade was said to be financed in sterling at that time.

It is the wide range of personal contacts which I remember with particular pleasure from my days in the department. My wife, like many Bank wives, bless them, dispensed hospitality to scores of visitors from Lagos, New York, St Helena or Pretoria. Our children soon learned that people are much the same, whatever continent they come from, and benefited from hearing first hand how tea is grown in Ceylon, or how you train cormorants to catch fish in Japan.

In Overseas such friendships had time to mature. It was not unusual to meet a Governor's PA in one decade, to encounter him as a head of department in the next, and in the fullness of time see him emerge as a Governor himself; and in between learn of his progress in the central banking network through mutual friends. In some countries progress up the ladder of success was swifter – offset only by the greater risk of being engulfed on the wrong side of a coup.

Our main task was the patient acquisition of detailed knowledge supplemented by regular visits by Advisers and

73

others to the groups of territories (or 'Parishes') for which they were responsible. Together they enabled us to speak with authority and be taken seriously by Whitehall departments, businessmen, journalists and all the other contacts (British and foreign) who brought such variety to the daily round

Latterly new circumstances have dictated new priorities. By 1995 detailed economic analysis was confined to the ten major countries. For the rest the Bank's resources were to be concentrated on two things: firstly, information to help strengthen banking supervision; and, secondly, training for personnel from young central banks, especially those in the former communist countries – for whom traditional central banking is like a voyage into uncharted waters.

Curiously, this latter activity almost brings the history of Overseas full circle. In the 1930's it first made its mark internationally through the work of Sir Otto Niemeyer and FFJ Powell in creating new central banks in Eastern Europe, Latin America and elsewhere.

I hope that our successors in the overseas intelligence-gathering business have as much fun as my generation did.

The Overseas Secondment

Overseas
Parthenia (Jacquie Pearce)

Let's drain a toast to Overseas!
The refuge of remote degrees,
The haunt of gifted amateurs
Whose elegance such use confers,
Engaged in training and research,
As Luther's Holy Roman Church.

Yet 'twould be churlish, all agree,
To doubt their versatility,
Whose itching pens can celebrate
The fall of bank, or interest rate,
Or deprecate from pole to pole
The failure of exchange control,
Or forecast Iceland's GDP
As erringly as HMT,
Assess the pros and cons of aid,
Miscalculate the terms of trade,
Add tome to tome on Ghana debt,
(It seems they haven't paid us yet),
Censure the crafty Japanese
For dumping ships beyond the seas,
Describe, in case you hadn't read it,
The Wonder Book of Export Credit,
Or failing more exotic pleasures,
Australia's new import measures,
The US soya export ban,
Investment in Afghanistan,
New lines of shipping (hello sailor!),
The cost of oil from Venezuela,
Bolivia's hyperinflation,

75

The mongu's third revaluation
Or Herstatt's road to liquidation;
Explain Peruvian brokers' fees,
How Sweden treats her employees,
The latest Eurodollar squabble,
How many drachmas to the rouble,
The role of peculating dagos,
Why concrete can't unload in Lagos,
Why Fiji's sugar's late this year,
Why Taiwan textiles disappear,
The flight of specie from Uganda,
Financial aims of Doctor Banda,
South African and Cyprus sherries,
Tax havens in the Grand Canaries
(Or was it Caymans?) – all, in short,
Of clear or tenuous import
To touch the interest of the Bank,
And buttress the Adviser's rank.
Here one his fertile brain expends
In macro-economic trends,
Bewitched by algebraic gnomics
Of monetary economics,
A tragicomical obsession
With multilateral regression.

Another sums, mustachios curling
Nigerian reserves in sterling,
One plans a Barmecidal feast
To pacify the Middle East;
His colleague tries to speculate
On Abu Dhabi and Kuwait.
The problem has a thousand facets –
How would the Saudis like their assets?

Recycling spreads its ghostly trammels;
We can't get by with dates and camels,
We'll have to offer something better –
A multipurpose carburettor?

Another pants to tell you why
The slump has passed Romania by,
The price of flats in Brussels squares,
Or what to do with Danzig shares,
The newest junta, coup or putsch,
(The climate seldom varies much),
Why chairman Mao is out of breath,
Our chances with the IMF,
Which banks are based in the Bahamas,
Why we import the worst bananas;
Do South Koreans profiteer?
How many Indians starved this year?
Can we decline to help the BIS?
Would Ziljstra take our views amiss?

Or would it cost a vast amount
To change the unit of account?
Depending whose advice you take,
We might be wise to join the Snake...

From Epitres d'Outremer (après Montesqieu), *published*
in The Old Lady *in* 1976

CHAPTER SEVEN

Travel Overseas

The Lament of the Bank Beadle, 1926

All sorts of curious folk
From all parts of the realm
Come here – and it's a joke
The awful yarns I tell 'em.

I asks 'em what they wants
And if they pause or mutter,
I take 'em by the pants
And slings 'em in the gutter.

Travel Overseas

'Merchants and Adventurers in all parts of the world' is how the Directors of the Bank of England were described in the first list of 1694. Even today those despatched overseas to uphold the Old Lady's DIET-A – Discretion, Integrity, Effectiveness, Tenacity and if possible, Acceptability – often face challenges.

Counterfeiting, forgery, pursuit of thieves, money-laundering and other criminal activity are one aspect of Bank travel overseas but there are other quality of life hazards on Bank trips when caught up in wars, revolutions, invasions, terrorist attacks, assassinations, kidnaps, hostage-taking, political turmoil, commercial mayhem and other forms of military and civil unrest.

The first Bank of England casualty overseas was the Deputy Governor in 1695. He had been delivering the wages of the British Army and had just arrived in the trenches at Namur alongside the King, who warned him to keep under cover. Too late – he had popped up to see what was happening and was promptly decapitated by a cannonball.

Throughout the last three centuries, there have been very many Bank travellers. In the 1960s and 1970s when I was a member of the Overseas Office, there were at any one time some thirty members of staff on overseas residential assignment and another twenty or so engaged overseas in routine 'parish-visiting', random 'fire-fighting' or occasional 'lamp-lighting'. Another ritual performed monthly since 1930 (with a brief interlude in 1939-45) has been the Governor's party, sometimes numbering five to eight, who have travelled with him to Basle for the monthly meetings of the Central Bank Governors in the Bank for International Settlements.

Out of these travels have come some exciting and astonishing stories. Take, for example, the escape of the Bank of England man in Kuwait during the Iraqi invasion and occupation in 1990. Following coded instructions on the BBC Overseas Service, he was hidden by Kuwaitis until he could be taken out by a group of friendly Iraqis – carefully concealed in a truck under a blanket covering a booty load of domestic refrigerators. By circuitous routes, on appalling road surfaces and through many road-blocks, he eventually reached safety in, of all least preferred destinations, the city of Baghdad. There help was waiting to hide him and transfer him safely to freedom.

'A Long Weekend in Algiers'

Christopher McMahon

The Chief Cashier and I, accompanied by our legal adviser, recently spent a long weekend in Algeria – it was first suggested to me by the US Ambassador in a telephone call at half-past seven on the morning of Friday 16 January 1981 and we were airborne from Heathrow at 11 am.

We were flown to Algeria with our American friends in a large US Airforce plane, comfortably fitted out with tables, chairs and beds. On the tables were ashtrays, radiating from which in star formation were strips of chewing gum. A particular feature of the plane was its entire lack of windows, which gave a sense of mystery to the undertaking from the start. The lack of windows also meant a rather severe jolt when we landed, quite unprepared.

We were whisked from the airport to the US Embassy in a motorcade of five black Fiats with police motorcycle outriders. As this proceeded at break-neck speed and with little regard for traffic regulations, or, indeed, traffic, down a long palm-lined avenue with the deep blue, deep sea harbour filled with large ships on one side, we felt rather as if we were behind the credits at the beginning of a wide-screen movie.

The US Embassy was one of three places in which we spent our entire time. The second was of course the British Embassy. It also had a beautiful garden with a fine view over the harbour, a swimming pool and tennis court and it was also a fantasy of a different kind, a late 19th century quasi-baronial structure with turrets and castellations which had at one time served as an English officers' club. Here, Sir Richard Faber presided over a calm that was in striking contrast to the bustle going on further up the hillside. We had comfortable bedrooms and breakfasted each morning on boiled egg, toast and delicious home-made marmalade from the orange-trees in the garden.

The rest of the time was spent in the Ministry of Foreign Affairs where we held all our discussions with three members of the Central Bank of Algeria (we never laid eyes on the Central Bank itself) mostly in a large conference room without windows which after some days was almost solid with smoke. Although the weather was beautiful – balmy, sunny days – we did not see much of it except that little patch of blue which negotiators call the sky.

And what were we actually doing from Friday until Tuesday evening? In essence, of course, our mission was simple: the Iranians were to hand over hostages and the Americans to hand over money. Since neither side was in direct contact with each other, with all negotiations being conducted through intermediaries, it was necessary for some institution to hold the 'stakes' and release them when the hostages were freed or return them if they were not. The size of the operation was daunting, involving as it did (even if only for a short time) a trebling of our (Bank of England) balance-sheet.

The certification process was completed at about 1.00 pm on the Tuesday and there followed the long nail-biting wait to see whether the hostages would be released and whether it would be before President Reagan's inauguration due at 5 pm (GMT = Algerian time). In fact the deadline was missed by about an hour and a half. It was not until about 6.30 pm that the three Algerian central bankers turned up at the British Embassy and formally delivered to me the message. I instructed the Bank to make payments. We then had a little celebratory whisky.

Finally we were privileged to see the hostages themselves. We went out to the airport with our American colleagues at around midnight and waited with suspense until the big plane landed. By that time it was raining but the hostages came down the steps and across the tarmac under the lights in apparent good spirits. A highly-coloured group with a number of red anoraks, they were all ushered into the airport lounge and welcoming speeches were made to them by the Minister of Foreign Affairs and Warren Christopher. It was very moving to see so quickly and so vividly the human result of all those arcane and detailed financial discussions.

The 66 members of the US Embassy staff had spent 444 days as hostages in Tehran prior to their release in Algiers.

Sir Christopher McMahon's account was first published in The Old Lady *in March 1981, from which, with his permission, these extracts have been taken.*

Sir Christopher (Kit) McMahon was Executive Director of the Bank of England in 1970-80, Deputy Governor in 1980-85 and Chairman and Chief Executive of Midland Bank in 1987-91. He describes his recreations as looking at pictures, buying books, going to the movies and helping in the garden.

Bank Serendipity

Jeremy Morse

Lloyds Bank plc
71,Lombard Street
London ECP 3BS
Chairman's Office

27th April 1990

Dear Paul,

In response to your appeal on page 32 of the March issue of *The Old Lady*, I have another Rupert Raw story for you which dates from the time after the sterling devaluation of November 1967.

Although there was no immediate rush by sterling area countries to move their reserves out of sterling, it was clear that their confidence had been fundamentally shaken. So early in 1968 we began to prepare plans for an orderly run-down, plans which eventuated that autumn in the negotiations for Sterling Agreements with more than 40 sterling area countries and associated support facilities from the G10 countries in Basle. Among those who developed the project were Roy Fenton, Eric Haslam, John Kirbyshire, Rupert Raw and myself.

By March we had worked out most of the problems posed by such a formidable negotiation, but there was one that we could not see our way through. At this point Rupert went for a skiing holiday, in the course of which he strayed far from the piste and fell into a deep circular crevasse.

The sides were sheer ice and he thought his end had come. But eventually he found that by cutting little ledges he could move up the sides on a slowly ascending spiral. After an hour or so, he judged that he was a quarter of the way. Suddenly he realised that safety was only a matter of time. His mind relaxed, and in the ensuing three hours before he reached the top, he cracked the problem of the Sterling Agreements which had been defeating us.

The incident seems to me to be typical of Rupert's dogged determination to get to the bottom (or top) of things. I hope you like it.

Yours sincerely,

Jeremy

Sir Jeremy Morse KCMG was an Executive Director of the Bank of England in 1965-1972 and a non-executive Director in 1993-97. He was Chairman of Lloyds Bank in 1977–93.

'British Rule Ends Tonight'
Peter Edgley

That had been the four-word banner headline in the Lagos *Daily Times* this morning. Now, at midnight, independence for Nigeria was only a minute away, and on the Lagos race-course, the Independence Tattoo was reaching its climax. We rose to sing 'God Save the Queen', and round us one could hear the cheerful murmurs of 'Last time, last time', but many thousands of African voices were joining in the singing. Then the lights were switched off for a few moments: and when they came on again, roars of cheering greeted the new green-and-white Nigerian flag flapping where the Union Jack had flown a few minutes before.

During my two years in Lagos, I saw the Central Bank of Nigeria evolve from scratch into a fully-fledged central bank with a staff of 160 occupying an imposing five-storey building. New Nigerian notes and coin were issued – £50 million of them – in exchange for the old West African currency previously shared with Sierra Leone, Gambia and the Gold Coast (in pre-Ghana days); and many other central banking functions – more important perhaps, but less spectacular – were undertaken. The launching of the Bank, in a matter of months from the arrival of a small Bank of England team about August 1958, supplemented later by Australian help, was a hectic experience but most satisfying to all who took part in it.

A group photograph of the Currency Office, taken soon after the Bank was opened, is before me as I write – 14 wide smiles, and an equal division between colourful robes and European lounge suits (mostly rather smarter than my own). As I look at the picture, the personalities come through. Here is our only Northerner, a dignified Hausa ploughing a lonely furrow among the noisy ebullient Ibos and Yorubas of the South. There is our young man-about-town and part-time singer in a local night-club. One face reminds me of endless political discussions; another of good-humoured arguments about 'bride-price' and its implications. A third recalls its owner's patient efforts to coach me in a few words of Yoruba. Here is our typist, whose wife made a beautiful costume for my four-year-old son; there our 'elder statesman', an inveterate organiser,who once inveigled ,me into sharing with Rex Akpofure, the Nigerian Keith Miller, the duties of MC at the annual dance of the Urhobo Students' Progressive Social Union.

Peter Edgley spent 30 years in Overseas Office, retiring as a Senior Adviser in 1986. Between 1958 and 1960 he was seconded to help set up the new Central Bank of Nigeria.

Brief for the Governor*

Visit of the Governor of the Central Bank of Atlantis for lunch at 12.30 on 16.10.69

The Bank has no major outstanding problems with Atlantis, all claims to sequestrated British property having now been abandoned.

The Governor was last entertained by HMG sixteen years ago and released last year.

Miss Bloggs, who first went to reorganise the Central Bank's filing system five years ago, was last heard of in the Governor's Personal Secretariat. She has not replied to any correspondence for the last twelve months. It might be considered offensive if we were to make direct reference to this, although it might be appropriate to offer a (younger) replacement.

It is traditional practice in Atlantis to conclude formal occasions such as this with the Atlantis National Anthem (*'May Pestilence Destroy the Imperialist British'*) to be sung by all to a tune vaguely akin to *'Three Little Maids from School are We'* and with the guests firing wildly into the air. The Messengers will feed the retainers and any pet dogs or snakes, and also keep everyone clear of the chandeliers.

* Drafted at an Overseas tea-party and submitted to The Old Lady *on 1.10.69 as spare* Flyleaf *material. The paragraph about Miss Bloggs was contributed by Alan Schofield. It was never published.*

Escape from Kuwait, 1990
Keith Wood

Outside, fighting could be heard all around, with heavy artillery and tanks in operation plus a great deal of small arms fire. The Kuwaiti border defences had clearly collapsed and given the Iraqis a free run of the city where they were mopping up the remaining pockets of resistance. It was already too late to make a run for the Saudi border as Kuwait's modern ring-road system had enabled the Iraqis to surround the city very quickly.

The army base, at the Ruler's Palace about 500 metres away, was under heavy attack and though common sense suggested staying indoors, curiosity is such that the view from the roof was far too engrossing to worry about what happened to the cat. The approach of about 25 helicopter gunships flying low over the house on their way to bomb the Palace tested my nerve, but still the fascination of hearing the explosions and watching the palls of smoke rise all around the city remained. The whole scene felt unreal almost as if I were watching a movie on TV.

The heavy guns had done their job and been replaced by small arms fire which seemed to be getting closer. I hid when a heavy lorry moved into the road, thinking it was the troops mopping up resistance from the houses, but felt a bit stupid when it turned out to be no more than the Korean dustmen cheerfully doing their morning collection.

The fight was not the exuberant type you've seen on television. I felt tremendous personal sadness as, I suspect, did the others leaving so many friends behind as well as feelings of guilt as to why I should have been so lucky. Fortunately, some weeks later, all the hostages were released, but still my Kuwaiti friends suffered as captives in their own country. None of us will ever be able fully to express our gratitude to them for feeding and protecting us during this time. It really is true that if you are a Kuwaiti's guest, he will give you everything that is his, even his life.

Keith Wood was seconded to the Central Bank of Kuwait in 1989-90. These extracts are taken, with the author's specific permission, from his article published in the Spring 1991 issue of The Old Lady *entitled 'Nothing Ever Happens in Summer'.*

Christmas in Bethlehem

Lawrence FT Smith

When we moved into our new Jerusalem home in early December 1997, the sound of the bells of the local church playing 'O Come all ye Faithful' drifted through the open windows – a welcome reminder that it was not long until the next big holiday, Christmas.

It was mid-December when we attended our first carol service, but people still seemed to be wishing us a 'Happy New Year and Merry Christmas' well into 1998. Indeed some Christmas decorations were permanent – we saw a shop-front painted with snow, tree and Santa in July when the temperature was over 100 degrees F.

Colleagues at the Palestine Monetary Authority urged that Christmas would not be complete without a visit to Bethlehem on Christmas Eve.

So on 24th December we set out for Bethlehem, which the Oslo Accords had put under the full control of the Palestinian Authority.

When we approached Bethlehem, we found ourselves facing large numbers of heavily armed troops and barriers closing the road. We later learned this was an annual occurrence – ensuring that whichever Jerusalem Patriarch or Bishop was scheduled to officiate could not get there on time. The long-suffering congregation was, however, inured to this and the service was simply put on hold until the officiating Bishop or Patriarch eventually did arrive. Suffice it to say that it was a day of great celebration – parades of scouts and other groups, marching bands, mounted police, colourful stalls.

Lawrence (known also as Tim, and earlier in his Bank of England career as Lefty) Smith was appointed Personal Assistant to the Managing Director of the International Monetary Fund in Washington DC and as First Secretary (Financial) in the British Embassy in Tokyo before becoming the Adviser covering the Middle East. After retirement in 1997 he completed two IMF assignments as General Policy Adviser to the Palestine Monetary Authority.

Dress Code at the New York Fed
Tim Porter

Business Casual

Men: Trousers (*e.g.* khakis, chinos, wide-wale corduroys), collared knit shirts (including polo-style shirts), sweaters, vests, socks, and covered-toe footwear (including loafers, boots, leather deck shoes). In general long sleeves are encouraged.

Inappropriate Dress

Men or Women: Warm-up or sweatpants, spandex, stretch pants without a long sweater, bib-overalls, baseball caps, tank tops, spaghetti-strapped dresses, mini-skirts, halter tops, shorts, bathing suits, beach sandals, ripped anything, extremely wrinkled anything.

Being back in Britain isn't bad. And some things in life are simpler: no bagels at all in the staff canteen, just plain and simple toast and butter.

Tim Porter was seconded to the New York Federal Reserve Bank in 2001–2. These extracts were taken, with his specific permission, from an article published in The Old Lady *in June 2002.*

New York Fed staff mostly adopt business casual attire, and here there is another confrontation with the American lexicon.

'It won't last – he's a Keynesian, she's a monetarist.'

The Accounts Course

Before me floats a sea of figures
The waves have washed my credits out
And the tide has drawn my debits in.

Angela Bailey, 1974

In Paradise by Nine

Here Lie the bones in kindly dark
Of Abel Burns, a humble clerk
Who fondly hopes with help divine
To be in Paradise by nine.

Anon, Our (Bank of England) Magazine 1884

I Shall Not Go to Tehran

I shall not go to Tehran
I cannot visit Timbuctoo,
It's questionable if I can
Run down to Plymouth or to Looe;
I'll spend my holidays at Kew
And sell my house and buy a hut,
This may seem singular to you.
Today my salary is cut.

J H McNulty, from the Ballade of Lost Delights

CHAPTER EIGHT

The Nightly Watch
Guarding the Gold

The Superintendent of the Watch

Beside the Tellers' Top Lock Key
  The Superintendent stands,
Under no circumstance he
  Must let it leave his hands

At length when dreary rounds are o'er
  To realms above he goes
And, glass in hand, proceeds to bore
  The Official with his woes

Until about 10.55
  His unreplenished glass
And colleague's yarns remind him that
  He needs must go, alas
To lock those massive gates through which
  No man, till morn, may pass

At dawn of day, or thereabouts,
  The bagpipes in the Yard
Announce, mid noisy oaths and shouts
  The passing of the Guard

Grumpy, dyspeptic, grizzling
  Back to his desk he goes
To while away the dreary hours
  Until the Bank shall close.

J H Ould 1932

The Nightly Watch
Guarding the Gold

To be or not to be on the Watch generally presented a dilemma. The privilege of achieving Administrative Rank in the Old Lady came with an invitation to look after her out of working hours. With the good news of promotion came a loss of freedom, amounting to losing one night a month, mutilating at least four weekends per year and rupturing one bank holiday in three. Ten years was considered a reasonable stint on the Watch. Woe betide the individual who declared that his own time with family and friends was worth more than donating – apart from a generous special Watch Allowance – 130 nights, a mere extra four months of one's life to the Governor and Company. In refusing, he could be no more sure of leaving an indelible mark on his record than if he had arrived before the Governors ten minutes late with mud on his boots and straw in his hair.

A Gentlemen's Club

On the upside, membership of the Watch opened up a new world of unexpected pleasures – those of a select, discreet and most comfortable gentlemen's club. The bedrooms had roomy mahogany panelled lockers and a wide variety of reading matter. The beds were well-sprung to cope with the more corpulent of our brethren with crisp white sheets and there were large, ancient baths with instant high-pressure water pumped from our own artesian wells and heated somewhere in the Bank's own power station throbbing deep down beneath our feet. The sitting-room bar was well-stocked. It catered for any colleagues who just happened to drop in between seven and seven-thirty each evening and any other officials who felt in need of a drink before going home or out to dinner or to the theatre or a concert.

The Official-in-Charge, Deputy and Superintendent-of-the-Watch then sat down in splendid style in the 'Golden Trough' Dining Room on the fourth floor to a delicious four-course dinner (and full lunch on Saturdays, Sundays and Bank Holidays) followed by a choice of brandy or port and a large Bank of England Havana cigar. Next door, in the evenings, the Officer of the Watch and his guest dined similarly but separately and were given in addition to their special Bank of England duty allowance, a half-bottle of brandy, which, if not consumed, usually left the Bank the following morning upright on top of the head clipped inside the bearskin.

The Bank Rules and Regulations stipulated that the Officer's guest had to be male, and many, therefore, were their girlfriends who turned up in jackets and trousers or kilts or other male attire. In my day, it was the Deputy Official's job to ensure that they were properly disguised on arrival and that they left in reasonably good order at the stipulated time.

A special rule came into force whenever the Gurkhas, each carrying a razor-sharp *kukri*, took over from the usual rotation of the five Guards Regiments. The Officials were instructed, whenever ordering the pursuit of a suspected interloper or stranger acting suspiciously, never to use the order 'Head off that man!'

Another delight was that the Official-in-Charge could invite his own family to tea in the Bank on Saturdays, Sundays and Bank Holidays between the hours of 3.00 pm and 5.00pm. While I was on the Watch from 1973 to 1981, my wife and children always took up the invitation, arriving promptly from nearby Greenwich and rarely leaving early. They developed their own Bank-related games and races and story-telling and the Chef never failed to produce delicate cucumber sandwiches, home-made cakes and specially delicious ice-cream. Big treats included visits to the Bank power-station, the Museum and the Court Room. When I moved on secondment for a year to Shell in 1976-77, my elder daughter, Clare, then six, had the greatest difficulty in understanding why she could not have tea at the weekend in Shell Centre.

A Para-Military Routine

The strict routine – para-military in character – began each night before six with the checking in of about a hundred keys, each part of a double, triple or quadruple control system. These were then deposited under dual control in the main key vault and the time lock set for the following morning. Only with the assistance of the City of London Police outside the Bank could access to the Vaults be obtained at night, by which time the whole Bank and Metropolitan Police HQ were on full alert. Early the following morning the process was reversed as the keys were signed out to the representatives of the various offices.

Dual control of all cash movements was instituted as early as 1801 after the Second Cashier had been convicted of embezzling half a million pounds. On one occasion – in 1819 – the main Bank keys were stolen from the Porter's Lodge at the Main Entrance. Other thefts followed elsewhere in the City and the police surveillance operation quickly identified the woman responsible and followed her back to her lodgings where they found a collection of 4000 keys stolen from public offices and City institutions. 'What a pity she was discovered' began one letter to *The Old Lady* 'If she had not been discovered, such a historically valuable collection of keys might have been preserved to this day'.

A final chore at 10.45 pm was to receive a report from the Security Control Room that the patrols had completed a thorough search of the building, a search, I recall, which one summer evening in 1980 produced a lady 'stagaire' from a Scandinavian central bank who, at 10.30 pm, was still sleeping off a special 'thank-you' luncheon she had organised for her Bank of England colleagues. At 11.00 pm the Official supervised the final locking and barricading of the double doors and entry hatch at the Front Entrance, rounding off the evening with a 'nightcap' and yet more chat and gossip with the Deputy before retiring happily to bed.

The Officials, Military Guard and Security Staff were not the only people in the Bank at night. Some nights when there was a financial crisis or restructuring of a city institution in trouble to be completed while the London markets were closed, parts of the Bank appeared busier than during the working day. On these occasions the Officials were active most of the night supervising the security aspects of the operation, taking in and forwarding urgent messages from central banks and others round the world, keeping senior management informed of what was going on and organising food hampers, beer and sandwiches and sometimes camp-beds and linen for everyone present. Most notable in my time were the various bank emergencies following the quadrupling of the oil price in October 1973, the takeover of Burmah Oil in December of that year and the overnight tripling of the Bank's balance sheet in 1981 when seized Iranian financial assets were used to secure the release of US Embassy hostages in Tehran after 444 days in captivity. Even today, in crises such as Northern Rock, work keeps large numbers of staff in the Bank until late at night.

Of Catapults and Cats

In the 18th and 19th Centuries, as many as eighty to ninety employees lived on the premises in Threadneedle Street, some on a permanent basis. The Chief Cashier (or later his

Deputy) and the Chief Porter continued the tradition up to the outbreak of war in 1914. Abraham Newland, Chief Cashier for 29 years from 1778 to 1807 – a busy time, what with the French Revolution and Napoleonic Wars – never spent a night outside the Bank in all his tenure of that office. Several children born in the Bank were recording their experiences during my early years in the Bank. They described the perambulators and nursemaids gathered beneath the old lime trees in the Bank garden with the older children roller-skating round the one-and-a-half miles of corridors, sliding down the banisters and playing Hunt the Ghost in the attics. Up on the roof in 1860, two small boys perfected a large catapult and succeeded in breaking the windows and skylights of the Britannia Life Assurance Society across the road in Princes Street.

Other occupants of the Bank have included a few horses to carry messengers. In 1803–4, in case an invasion by the French might necessitate the transfer of the gold, notes and ledgers to the safety of a large house which had been purchased near Monmouth, contractors were on notice to supply 66 8-horse heavy wagons, each capable of carrying over two tons. In the Bank, the bullion was ready to be transported packed and marked carefully in wooden crates. The order to move was never given. Victory at Trafalgar in October 1805 removed for ever the threat of another French invasion. But in 1940 several departments of the Bank including that of the Chief Accountant were evacuated lock, stock and barrel to Whitchurch and adjacent villages in Hampshire.

There were also the bees belonging to Lord Kingsdown, (Governor 1983-93), all hived on the roof and producers of a speciality, City of London Honey. During the Second World War, 1939-45, a lively trade in the garden and small-holding produce of the staff developed, particularly fruit, vegetables, eggs, pies, cakes as well as rabbits, hens and ducks and there were stories from Securities Office of how, for example, a crate of live Rhode Island Reds was opened surreptitiously as a prank. All escaped, scattering loose papers and perching high up out of reach, causing consternation when their own deposits were discovered in the open ledgers on the desks below. A group of Bank fisherman smuggled live chub into the Bank and installed them in the Bank fountain where they survived for several years. There was also a colony of Bank cats, charged with keeping the rodent population at bay and until the 1890's enjoying their own official victualling allowance. In 1980 the Officials were asked to refrain from bringing their own dogs on the Watch after an elderly and incontinent St Bernard, which could not be left alone at home, had relieved itself repeatedly in the Garden Court.

Whatever the eccentricities and private passions and enthusiasms of the Officials-in-Charge – that happy band of collectors of butterflies, restorers of antiques, breeders of pigs, constructors of model steam engines, historians of the obscure and experts in the unusual – their talk together over breakfast, coffee, lunch, tea and dinner and much of the time between with the messengers, engineers, security staff and others revolved around Bank stories, Bank characters and City gossip. It was a delicate, leisurely trading of rumour, information and opinion. A random, old-fashioned, casual process, you might think, as you might find in a regimental officers' mess or on Royal Navy ships at sea or in a Pall Mall club. But it was also a management training scheme, which, at negligible cost to the Bank, welded middle management into a team where, after several years, each knew the rest remarkably well. Shaken out of the daily commute, there was a chance to stand back regularly once a month with excellent food and a rotation of good company from all parts of the Bank to reflect and talk things through, a regular refreshing of the spirit and release from any tension, frustration or irritation.

Mr Smith and Mrs Brown

Of all these stories I collected from the Watch, may I whet your appetite with one from the nineteen-thirties. For reasons of Bank discretion, let us call them Mr Smith and Mrs Brown. Mrs Brown arrived early one December morning not long after her husband's funeral. She was tidily and severely dressed in black. The Chief Gatekeeper expressed his condolences and summoned a spare Deputy Principal, Mr Smith, who introduced himself and escorted Mrs Brown to one of those spotless Bank waiting-rooms where the latest copy of *The Old Lady* vied for attention with the day's *Financial Times*. Mrs Brown produced a bunch of keys and asked whether she might be allowed to remove her husband's personal belongings from his locker in the Officials' quarters. After his ten years on the Watch, she expected to pick up his pyjamas, slippers and dressing-gown as well as his stock of cigars.

Smith ordered coffee for her and, knowing a tale or two about what might or might not be found in the locked personal lockers of members of the staff, he took the keys and offered to bring down everything he could find. He half expected to find Brown – *Old Misery*, they used to call him – sitting there waiting for him, tapping precisely and impatiently, as was his habit, with a one-foot wooden ruler.

Entering the half-moon staircase in the North East corner of the Bank, Smith circled the large studded treasure chest where, from 1694, the infant Bank used to lock up its valuables overnight, past the sign to the Medical Quarters, where used to stand a venerable wheel-chair, labelled on one occasion, I remember, by one wag *For the Use of the Governors Only*.

None of the keys on the bunch fitted any of the locks. Smith checked through the current and past rosters carefully. There was no mention of any Mr Brown. A telephone call to Establishments confirmed the indisputable fact for the full period over the past ten years. He returned slowly, taking time to choose his words carefully. His answer in Bank style, had to be perfectly accurate. Clear diction. Short sentences. No time to be interrupted. No offence to be given:

'No. Mrs Brown, there are none of Mr Brown's belongings in the Officials' Quarters.'

He handed back the bunch of keys. 'Good-bye Mrs Brown and good luck!'

Gone for Ever

All of this in the Bank has now vanished. The role of the Superintendent-of-the-Watch was phased out in 1973-4 more or less at the same time as the abolition of the Military Guard which had performed its duty every night in war and in peace since the Gordon Riots in 1780. The rot set in with the laudable and courageous appointment, for the first time, of a Lady of the Watch resulting in a straw poll of the wives of the Officials who proved unanimous in their disapproval. Today, the role is performed by highly professional full-time Security Officers, elaborate, instantaneous electronics, surveillance cameras and mobile phones. Gone, for ever, are those jolly evenings and that magnificent *camaraderie*.

Guarding the Gold

Central Banks are notorious for not divulging precise numbers concerning their operations – unless absolutely necessary. Market values change from year to year, from month to month, from week to week, from minute to minute. Who can predict what the future will hold? So any statistics on a given day will be out-of-date and incorrect within a day or two and may become highly misleading. Why bother?

What can be said with certainty about the gold in the vaults of the Bank of England is that there is a lot of it (that held by the Bank as custodian totalled £43 billion at end 2007). This may be more than that in Fort Knox and may be less than that in the Federal Reserve Bank of New York, the other two locations generally assumed to be in the top three. There are big differences between them. Fort Knox is simply a large, heavily-protected depositary in open country. The gold in the Bank of England belongs mainly to other people – other central banks and the operators on the London-based global gold-market. So the working stores of the Bank bullion vaults are constantly being tinkered with as traded gold is moved from one low pile to another. The piles are kept low on account of weight restrictions. If the gold bars were to be placed in piles as high as in the New York Fed where they rest on the bedrock of Manhattan, the whole store in London might be in danger of vanishing suddenly through the vault floor into the mud and alluvial silt of the Thames Basin. In Paris I have enjoyed the surprising experience of passing through massive gold vault doors after taking the quite long elevator ride down to where the French gold sits in vaults carved into the bedrock below the Seine alluvial mud and silt. In Dubai, part of my responsibility in 1970-71, I have often watched lines of men in white *dishdashas*, filing onto the smuggling dhows for India, each carrying one or two standard gold bars newly arrived from London or Johannesburg or Vladivostok, with not a single guard in sight.

The Bank is still silent on the story of the sewage engineer who in the early nineteenth century was surveying the underground channels of the River

Walbrook which runs alongside the Bank and then partly under the Bank. At one point late at night he found rotten floor boards above his head and poked his way through to find himself in the main gold vault. He retraced his steps and that evening delivered a letter by hand to the Governor inviting him to send officials to meet him in the Gold Vault at a certain hour the following day. The Bank took the invitation seriously and were there to meet him as he emerged through the hole in the floor. A search through the Bank archive of the period produced a payment which may or may not have been a reward for his honesty.

The Bullion Office has a string of stories about lost shipments of gold over the years. In October 1799 the bank consigned £350,000 in bullion to Hamburg. Most of it was carried on the frigate *La Lutine*, which sank in a storm off the Dutch island of Texel. Only the ship's bell was recovered to be hung prominently at Lloyds where it is rung on the news of any major shipping disaster. In 1917, the *Laurentic*, carrying £5,000,000 in gold to support the pound on the New York exchange market, was torpedoed and sunk off Donegal. In 1940, the Bank shipped £2,500,000 of gold to the USA on *HMS Niagara*, which hit a mine and sank in 438 feet. Divers recovered 94 per cent of the gold in 1941 and the full story appeared in book form in *Gold from the Sea* by James Taylor.

In 1938-1941, large shipments of gold bullion began arriving at British ports, all destined for the Bank of England. Much of it came by courtesy of the Royal Navy in conditions of the strictest secrecy. Robert Stevenson told of reporting, as instructed by the Bank, to the Harbour Master at Gourock. It was a cold dark winter's night. He was told that a tender was waiting for him at the end of the pier. Robert had no idea which ship he was meeting and, as a central banker, knew better than to ask. He set out into the night down the pier ideally camouflaged in his dark City suit, black bowler and clutching his tightly furled black umbrella.

At the end of the pier he was surprised to find two young boys sitting in a small dinghy with an outboard. He climbed down a long vertical iron ladder and they set off into the pitch-black night, just about holding their own against a strong spring tide. The Luftwaffe arrived overhead for their nightly raid and, in the flashes and explosions, he could make out dozens of vessels at anchor with all lights extinguished.

'Which ship?' asked the elder boy. No, he had not been told. He had simply been told to take the gentleman wherever he wanted to go. At this point the outboard engine spluttered and died. The boys struggled with it but with no result.

'Look out!' shouted the younger boy. The dinghy was being swept down onto the protruding bow of a sunken destroyer. The motor refused to start. They shot past at some speed and out into the open waters of the Clyde.

Several hours later, all three were returned to Gourock Pier. The Harbour Master congratulated the boys. 'What do you think you were doing out there?', he asked Robert. They set off again at once, this time with an armed escort. A Royal Navy launch was waiting and the mission was quickly accomplished and the gold delivered safely and in good order through the Bank of England Bullion Gate at the back of the Bank in Lothbury.

Another gold story dates from the time when transfers of up to five or six gold bars could be made more easily and more discreetly by chartered bi-plane without the formalities of the cross-Channel sea ferries where any such transfer might attract unwelcome attention. The Bank of England man would sit in the passenger seat next to the pilot with the gold bars on the floor between them. On this occasion the engine failed somewhere over Kent and an emergency landing took place in a meadow close to an isolated farm-house. The jolt of the touchdown was enough to dislodge the gold which slid backwards down the cabin. The aircraft brakes were inadequate to halt the plane in time and it ended up nose-down in the farmer's pond. The gold had been shot forward between them with some momentum. It had passed straight through the front of the aircraft and had vanished beneath the murky waters of the pond. The pilot and the Bank man climbed out unharmed and were immediately confronted by the farmer, somewhat irate.

'What are you doing in my pond?' he asked. The merest thought of compensation was already heavy in the air.

The pilot was silent. 'We lost our ballast' said the Bank of England man.

'No worry!' beamed the farmer. 'I can let you have some more for a tenner. I will go and get it in the trailer and pull you out with the tractor.'

As soon as the farmer had gone, they both jumped waist-deep into the pond, found all the gold and had restowed it safely out-of-sight in the cabin before he reappeared. The danger was over.

'Sometimes I think he doesn't panic in a crisis and sometimes I think he doesn't give a damn.'

A Bank-Club Salad

I cannot sing the old songs now —
In sooth, I quite forget 'em
And so to-night I make my bow,
And hope you'll not regret 'em;

I'll sing a song of money-bags,
A little clerkly ballad:
A thing you'd call, you funny wags,
A sort of 'Bank-Club Salad'.

Anon, A Ballad of Bankdom
Published in the Bank of England, 1884

If I Built A Bank for You, Dear

If I built a Bank for you dear,
Just a Bank for me and you
We'd arrive at half-past ten, dear
And leave again at two
With at least three hours for luncheon
In the Bank I built for you.

Fortunello, 1922

The People of the Bank

How many teeth to the ceaseless stones?
How many lives to the flood?

Our (Bank of England) Magazine, 1884

109

CHAPTER NINE

The Old Lady at Play

The Bank of England
Sports Club is
100 Years Old

A View of Bank of England Cuisine

If you can force your teeth through bone and sinew
Until your plate is clear and all is gone,
And still with interest peruse the menu
And hesitate but still eat on.

If you can see, all grumbling means time wasted,
And say aloud, when everything goes wrong,
'This food's the best that I have ever tasted,'
Yours is the courage which makes empires strong.

J H McNulty, 1922 If – Mr Kipling Visits the Club

The Bank of England Sports Club
A Jewel in the Crown

Peter J Bull

*I*n my younger days it used to be said that one did not have to have any qualifications to do any job in the Bank: one was simply expected to get on and do it, and if one did well one might move on to something else, and if not one would join the multitude of rather disappointed gentlemen of the Bank and channel one's energies into more personal interests. That attitude was not without some benefit because some individuals rose to the challenge in many fields, some even around the globe, and many eventually turned out to be able to tackle any problem or situation with some credit. And that was one of the great virtues of the Bank: it produced more rounded people who could turn their hand to almost anything with some measure of success.

In those days it seemed to help if one did sport. It used to be cynical to say that to have been to a good school, have some charm and play cricket was an essential qualification for promotion in the Bank. I was obviously doomed to get nowhere but my closest friend came to my rescue:

'You've got to do some sport on Saturday afternoons', he said, 'and as I am going to do cross-country you have got to do cross-country too'

And so I made my first visit to the Bank's Sports Club for an afternoon of self-inflicted torture.

Most people worked on Saturday mornings, and there was lunch at Tokenhouse Yard and the teams set off for their games, those going to the Club by taking a train to Barnes via Waterloo, as very few had cars. Saturday's sport was a ritual, and some of the senior echelons of the Bank were regular participants, like Leslie O'Brien, Jasper Hollom and George Blunden: some people thought that being seen at the Sports Club was a key to a successful career.

For some masochistic reason I kept up the running and eventually became quite philosophical about it, partly because it got me out of the all too sporty atmosphere of the Club into the beauty of Richmond Park, which even on wintry days was a joy. And the evenings provided an antidote in the form of good company and good cheer.

Although I have had a stab at most ball games I was never good at any, partly because I could never see the ball quickly enough. So I became an athlete. I was persuaded to be the Secretary of the Athletic Section. At around that time the Sports Club invested in a pole vault and landing pit but there was no one to use it. So I was delegated to become a pole-vaulter. I do not think I ever cleared two metres, but I did once score for the Bank.

The only thing I was proud of at that time was when on holiday in Paris in September 1952 I went into the Banque de France and asked to see the Secretary of their Athletic Section. He was duly produced and I invited them to send a team to compete in 1953 in what is now called Open Day, and that led to a cross-country match in Paris in January 1955. Those were amongst the first inter-central bank fixtures in the post World War Two years. I somehow believed in developing closer personal relations between people in central banks, and still do, although I now feel that the cultural differences between the peoples of some major nations will always impede pie-in-the-sky ideas like a common foreign policy and that it is only by recognising and not trying to change one's national identity that one can try to gain an international dimension.

No one would ever have said that I was sporty but one day I was approached to stand for the Chairmanship of the Sports Club and, improbably, I found myself elected. That was another job for which I had hardly any qualifications. True, I had been on the General Committee in the early 1950's when the rebuilding of the Men's Pavilion was being planned but at that time I was regarded by the pre-War members as a nuisance for not wishing to recreate the pre-War Pavilion which they loved, and not one of my 'modern' suggestions was accepted. In those days before the rebuilding, the men changed in the repaired remains of the bombed building, the iron frame of which is now hidden behind what is the present dining room. The women changed in their pavilion – Redgates Lodge – where we all had tea, with the bar in the side-lounge. The idea of amalgamating the Men's and Women's clubs was then out of the question. When the new Pavilion was opened in 1956 women were allowed in only after 8.00 pm on a Saturday evening. A hatch under the round staircase gave them access for drinks and enabled them to hear some of the Rugby songs – which may have been educational. It fell to me – a bachelor – to propose the amalgamation of the two clubs in, I think, 1970 and later to open the Club to the non-banking staff and introduce family membership.

The Club's 75th Anniversary history records the debt owed to Governor Leslie O'Brien who got the Court of Directors to agree to the building of the Swimming Pool and Sports Complex and the modernisation of the pavilion despite the economic crisis at that time. He also initiated the clearing of some of the shrubs around the azaleas and rhododendrons to create a picnic area that is still a stretch of glorious colour in the Spring.

I do not think that adequate tribute has been paid to Jasper Hollom, nor to George Blunden who allowed the Club to keep the bar profits, thus transforming our financial position and helping so many more central bank and other tours to be undertaken. Also, when his successor wanted to stop some new projects at the Club he told him bluntly that he had already approved the expenditure before he ceased to be the Deputy Governor. The full extent of the support given by Governor Leigh-Pemberton was also exceptional, and Eddie George and Mervyn King have carried on the good work.

Montagu Norman used to visit the Club on Sports Days before the war but I believe that active day-to-day gubernatorial support only goes back to the days of Lord O'Brien, although Lord Cobbold was an occasional visitor and Sir Cyril Hawker was sometimes at Roehampton playing cricket. We have been very lucky over the years with support from the top – people who have understood the wider value of the Sports Club.

In my earliest days in the Bank, I never thought that running would transform my life. It is a very therapeutic form of relaxation, and I have run with pleasure on my travels, sometimes on bank business, in many cities across the World. A very good friend who was a surgeon once said to me, 'If you get home in the evening and feel very tired go out for a run and you will come back refreshed and relaxed and have a much better sleep.' And so it has been.

Moreover, sometimes at the end of a busy day when I had a difficult problem to find an answer to I would go out for a run and the solution would come.

'One thing about Committees, they take your mind off the work.'

The Club for Bad Players

'Finally, I told Mr Hoare that the subs must be cheap as fellows lived all over London. Secondly, the club must be for bad players because good ones could always get a game.'

AES Curtis, first Honorary Secretary of the Bank of England Sports Club, 1908 who had collected within the Bank the first 250 signatures in support of the idea.

Wild Thyme

I know a Bank: but it is not
The bank which Oberon describes
Where Queen Titania forgot
In blissful sleep, his diatribes.

The Bank I know is not for sleep,
Men go and work there day by day
No wild thyme blows; no flowers peep;
Nor ever there do fairies play.

W Marston Acres, 1927

A Round-Bottom Decanter

Graham Dunbar

In the 1950s the Old Lady resumed sporting contacts with Central Banks across the Channel, initially with the Soccer and Rugby fraternities. At home, the Sport Club entertained on a proverbial shoe-string budget until it was realised that our friends abroad were treating these meetings with full Central Bank hospitality.

I can recall many unusual incidents, as when, at a soirée in Brussels, our Chairman (Denis Brookes) invited the wife of the Governor of the Banque Nationale de Belgique to dance, only to be declined with great courtesy and the words:

'I think not now as the Band are playing the Belgian National Anthem.'

On the home front, there were numerous Easter tours, but it was the Golfing Society who ventured north of the border where they developed a strong rapport with the Bank of Scotland; this lasts to the present day with an annual contest for the 'Auld Banks' Cup'.

During one of these meetings, lunch in the Directors' Mess at the Mound in Edinburgh concluded with the port being passed round in a beautiful cut-glass decanter which had a rounded bottom. This had recently been presented by a retiring member of the Mess who had been greatly frustrated by the port coming to all too frequent stops on the way round.

Happy memories and many long-lasting friendships – which can only be good!

'Wow! What Excitement, What Anticipation!'

A Britannia Club Outing, 1921

And so it was on the sixth day of the week when all those that laboured were wearied exceedingly and those that laboured not were well nigh sleeping, that one among them said unto those that were with him:

'Let us go hence towards Preston and then let us hold forth among ourselves in feats of skill that those who see may marvel muchly.'

And they came unto the borders of Preston which is beyond Wembley but a strange land to some. And their thirst was sore so that with one accord they sought out a damsel bearing many pitchers of liquid and were refreshed.

And when they had all drunk, they clad themselves in white apparel and coats of many colours, showing how they had once suffered captivity and they divided themselves into bands and cast lots.

And one band took missiles and threw lustily at their opponents, who said:

'Let us guard ourselves against hurt, lest some ill befalls us.'

Whereat these last gathered themselves weapons of willow wherewith to defend themselves.

The battle lasted until the setting down of the sun. And many and divers were the ways that they returned to their homes – some by circuitous routes as men in a dream, some with halting feet and others crying for guidance, and the dust lay heavily upon them. Notwithstanding they came into their own tents. And their fame spread before them and much thereof is written in the book of Britannia.

From *The Britannia Quarterly*, August 1921

'Something Uniquely English'
Squash – The Central Bankers' Game
1980

Gordon Richardson

…It is ten years since Lord O'Brien opened the sports hall and swimming pool. One must confess that these courts are not built on quite the same ample, not to say, magnificent scale as that other complex. Indeed the comparison perhaps symbolises all too well the contrast between the harder and more constrained world of today and the world of 1970 when oil cost two dollars a barrel, compared with 30 dollars or more today…

Speaking more specifically of these courts, it seems to me that it is particularly apt that the latest expansion of the Club should take this form. For Squash should surely be the Central Banker's game par excellence. It appeals to his instincts in more than one respect. First, it is economical of resources – employing only two people, who play very hard for a short period, expend only human – and not significantly OPEC – energy and who then pass the court on to other players. I have reluctantly to accept a certain contrast in this respect to cricket which occupies great tracts of land and in which 22 people are nominally employed, but where restrictive practices prevent more than two from working together – or against each other – for most of the time, while the others stand or sit around idly. Second, the game should attract the Central Banker's admiration because Squash, like the City of London, depends largely on self-regulation. Just as in this country we have no bank inspectors and no SE, so Squash players generally sort out their differences without need for the referee's whistle or the umpire's white coat – although this is not to say that animated disputes never occur either on court or in the City. Perhaps the City should evolve some way of diffusing disputes analagous to asking for a 'let'.

There is, I am bound to say finally, one point on which a Central Banker might have some reservation. Whereas Fives was invented as boys hit balls at some buttresses of Eton College Chapel, it is said that Squash was developed among the debtors locked up in the Fleet Prison. But the game has long thrown off any implication of 'rackets' (in the Chicago sense) and these new courts are a recognition of its present astonishing popularity.

From a speech on the opening of the new Bank of England Sports Club Squash courts on 13th July 1980 published here with the specific permission of Lord Richardson, who was Governor 1973–1983.

Golf – A Perfect Round

He found it easier to pray,
In God's fresh air, he'd always say
And meant by this, it would appear,
The golf-links' atmosphere.

The air most welcome to his soul
Blew strongly round the nineteenth hole,
Where every Sabbath he would sit,
Communing with the Infinite.

Now he, at last, has surely found
In Heaven above a perfect round.

From *More Bank of England Epitaphs, Anon*

Soccer – Veteran Ace

There is never a lack of endeavour.
Though there is sometimes a shortage of pace.
But in the area he's still the governor,
When the crunch comes, still the team's ace.
No young striker can claim the advantage.
But before the first touch on the ball
He may think the old lad is long past it
And shouldn't be playing at all.
But after the first bruising tackle
When he's picked himself up off the floor
He will know there and then who's the master
And that he's unlikely to score…

Michael Carter, 2002

Lacrosse – Swing the Ball

Voices bright and the shadows black,
Cecily, Margaret, Paul
And dancing out their secret track
They sing and circle, circle back
And fling and swing the ball

Joan Bridges, 1953

Tennis – Mixed Doubles

Mankind, you're all like Mother Eve!
What's yours can never please you
In secret trees the serpents weave
False tales of joy to tease you
'Give us forbidden fruit!' you yell;
'Without it, paradise is hell'.

CA Gunston, 1933

Bird-watching

The bird life around Hesketh was varied and impressive
for those who understood such things. Brookes on one of
his many forays into the surrounding countryside put up
on one shot, ten shelducks, two widgeon, a curlew and a
flock of little ringed plovers. The lapwings, being made
of sterner stuff, stayed to watch his fruitless search.

Alan May: From The Bank Golfing Society's Lancashire Tour, *published in* The Old Lady, *September 2002*

Disappearing Over the Horizon

The Editor no doubt feels that the first man to enter the Bank as a nineteen year-old probationer and to finish being Governor ought to have something to say. I hope he is right… I do not feel very inspired.

In any case the readers of The Old Lady may well feel that the sight of me disappearing over the horizon on one of my hobby-horses is not their idea of a fond farewell. So let me say simply how grateful I am to my colleagues past and price for the good life they have given me in a community where good manners have always prevailed and culture was not a dirty word, where discipline was accepted as conducive to good order and efficiency and where intellectual effort was encouraged at all times…

Leslie O'Brien, Governor 1966–73, quoted at the Annual Threadneedle Club Dinner in 1987.

In The Old Lady *issue where the above appeared in 1973, JV Bailey added a footnote:*

'*On his sporting prowess one is bound to drop to a lower key. He has been described as a crafty tennis player – which might be interpreted as Not Actually Cheating. But his election to membership of The All England Club presumably implies an unblemished record.*'

Netball
Stephanie Robinson

Dear Diary,

Sorry. Haven't written for ages. Been really busy. Loads to tell you. Only a couple more games before the season ends. I expect I'm not the only one glad the season's drawing to a close – not sure how SuperTrace manages to 'magic' teams out every week. Perhaps she'll hibernate this summer? Will be good to have free Thursday (late-night shopping) and Saturdays again.

May 2002   Meghan's announced she's expecting her first baby so can't play in the summer league (understandable) and hopes to be back on court by the end of next season (very dedicated!)…

June 2002   More baby news. Must be something in the air. Teresa from our FSA contingent has announced that she is expecting her first baby. Hope it's not catching. League results have arrived. Not at all bad… Seems that it is catching. Michele Davenport (née Cave) has announced the arrival of her second baby…

July 2002   I've just remembered now why I play netball! To escape housework. At least there's a netball weekend on the horizon.

September 2002   The annual meeting and then training – sounds an ideal time to go on holiday. But by missing the AGM I found on my return that I had been voted in to submit reports for *The Old Lady*. There are more babies about. Gina Wooderson (Dorset contingent) has announced that she is expecting her second baby. Guess she won't be driving up from Dorset to be on court this season.

From Sports Report – NETBALL – A season in the life of Fidget Bones by Stephanie Robinson published in The Old Lady, *December* 2002.

What it all Stands For

Robin Leigh-Pemberton

Long before I became Governor I had heard about the Bank of England Sports Club and had had the pleasure of playing against visiting Bank teams. But when my wife and I saw Roehampton for the first time we were both impressed by the excellence of the facilities and the quality of the grounds. We were able to appreciate in a small way the atmosphere to which many generations of Bank sportsmen and sportswomen have contributed and also to feel something of what it all stands for.

From the President of the Bank of England Sports Club's Forward to THE HOUSE, *a history of the first* 75 *years of the BESC dated February* 1984

Lord Kingsdown, Governor 1983–93.

Cricket is not my Thing'
Pamela Clayton

Cricket is not my thing. I can take it or leave it. Mostly I leave it. This is not because of my ignorance of the game. Unlike Lawrie Lee I cannot recall my childhood with clarity and beauty from the age of three, but I do remember a patch of green, worn down so that it looked like brown unpolished lino, a yellow fire hydrant marker used as a wicket and the slap of rubber ball on a copper stick.*

We girls were only allowed in the game as deep fielders and this meant standing in the hedges to stop the ball from smashing the windows of the houses around. We were frequently unsuccessful and the tinkle of glass was the signal to bolt for it. I marvel at the forbearance of the grown-ups in those days. I can only conclude that, as we were at war, they didn't care much about their windows; if we didn't break them, then the Germans would (and did).

*The stick or baton was made of wood (not copper) and was used to stir the 'copper', the cylindrical metal drum used in most homes to launder the family's dirty clothes in hot, soapy water.

Billiards

Goosey goosey gander
Whither shall I wander?
Down to Roehampton,
And on the Club veranda,
There I met a solemn man
With cuffs upon his feet,
I took him to the billiard room
And made him stand me treat…

From More Old Lady Nursery Rhymes, Anon, 1922

Rowing

Taffy was a Senior Clerk,
Taffy was a swank,
Taffy seemed to think that he
Had bought the blooming Bank,
Taffy took a month's G.L.,
And floated on the ocean,
Now he's on the floating list,
  And bang goes his promotion

From More Old Lady Verse, Anon, 1932

Dancing – Do You Miss Me?

Will you still be young and pretty,
When I meet you once again?
Connie, Chris, Camilla, Kitty,
Will you still be young and pretty,
When at last I leave the City
By my pre-Conversion train?

Do you miss me in the dances
I so often danced with you?
Fay, Felicity and Frances,
Do you miss me in the dances?
Or have someone else's glances
Led to your conversion too?

When the Powers-that-be shall free me
(Day of happiness, sublime!),
Maisie, Mollie, Myra, Mimi,
When the Powers-that-be shall free me
When, or rather if, you see me
Will you share my overtime?

Magog 1933

Sometimes, urgent work demands in the Bank seriously disrupted the weekend match programme at the Sports Club. The 5% War Stock conversion operation for example took 750 members of the Bank staff from 30th June to 6th August 1932. Everyone on overtime at the Bank was, of course, well compensated, safely transported and well-fed and refreshed at all times. In his official report to the Bank, Henry Jacobs, Manager of the Bank of England Club pointed out that in total 119,276 special luncheons and dinners had been served within that period. One meal consumed three quarters of a ton of salmon and another, 700 carcases of lamb and 2000lb of fresh peas were shelled on the premises in one day. The totals for the period included 15 tons of Scotch Beef, 1000 Lobsters, 4422 chickens, 2703 ducks, 3456 gallons of draught beer and 50 tons of potatoes. One hundred and ninety one extra waitresses were hired.

Vintage Hoffmann

Barry Hoffmann

I can endeavour to clarify the 'up-the-hill/down the hill' bowling conundrum at St Lawrence. The contours of the ground are such that you have to run uphill to bowl at the end where the wicket slopes downhill and run downhill at the end where the wicket slopes uphill. Just to add to the entertainment the wicket also slopes from side to side, as at Lords.

It was encouraging to see the Tour in good health in its 81st year. At one stage there were sixteen players available on each of the first two days before a certain natural erosion set in.

From The Old Lady, *December 2002*

Barry Hoffmann was a regular and much savoured Sports Correspondent of The Old Lady *from 1960.*

More Vintage Hoffmann

It is with a certain amount of sadness that I have to report that our hopes of promotion have been unfulfilled, a slow start to the season and lack of regular appearances by some members of the higher sides being the main causes. Our efforts have not been entirely in vain, however, for we managed to score 100 goals much to our delight and eventual relief. A bottle of champagne was rather optimistically bought after we had scored 92 goals, but this only seemed to cast an evil influence over our play. After a rather lengthy spell maturing at the bottom of a football bag, however, it was finally broached.

One is left with the hope that next season we may fight harder and obtain our just reward, whatever that may be.

From The Old Lady, June 1961

Even More Vintage Hoffmann

I have noticed over the years, when captaining a side, that there is a certain deviousness that some bowlers adopt on being asked from which end they wish to bowl. Some are sufficiently good that they have no need to be underhand; they merely inform you which end they have chosen. Their choice, however, normally depends on any slope – perceived or otherwise, which way the wind is blowing and the relative size of the boundaries. One legendary Bank bowler sometimes had to pull out his handkerchief to ascertain the direction of the wind. We, of course, could do likewise but his handkerchief invariably blew in the opposite direction from ours.

From The Old Lady, December 2002

'A Bit of Tennis'

Mervyn King

Addressing the 17th Annual Dinner of the Threadneeedle Club on 13th November 2002 just prior to the announcement of his appointment as Governor,* Mervyn King responded to Jonathan Charkham's introductory remarks by quoting Paul Volcker on the art of central banking as 'reliance on a mystique'. He traced, with the sporting idiom and metaphor to be expected of an Aston Villa supporter, the enhanced visibility of the last five years and the Bank's success in not only staying within the government guidelines, but also in defending the city goal-posts and sharing the underlying game-plan with the press and the public.

On assuming office on 1st July 2003, Mervyn King was widely reported in the Press as hoping to attend fewer dinners than his predecessor:

> *'I may not go to as many in order to leave time for playing a bit of tennis…'*

Skating

Geoffrey Yates

Geoffrey Yates, an Assistant Hon Sec in the Welfare Office, requested leave in 1936 'to do a bit of skating'. He represented Great Britain in the 1936 Winter Olympics at Gharmisch-Partenkirchen.

Security at the stadium was so tight that, one day, the British team were denied entry as Herr Hitler was paying a visit. Circling the stadium, they found at the back a train standing in a siding which led into the stadium. Yates and his team climbed in at the far end, and proceeded to walk through the full length of the train, passing Feldmarschall Goering slumped in a chair deep in slumber. As they stepped down, they were greeted warmly by a band and also, at the foot of the steps by Adolf Hitler himself who thanked them for their visit and shook hands with them in turn.

Overheard Outside the Sports Club Bar

'I'll come to the Saturday night dance if I have
nothing on.'

'What kind of a husband do you advise me to get?'
'Get a single man and leave the husbands alone.'

'In sickness and in health, through cricket and through soccer.'

'What is the meaning of the word matrimony? Father says it isn't a
word; it's a sentence.'

Playing the Game – By Our Rules

Garth Hewitt

Governor's Day

SUNSHINE, summer finery, Pimms, celebrity cricketers, lawn tennis, cold Scottish salmon, parfait, chilled wine, cream teas, – Governor's Day at the Bank of England Sports Club – the Bank's very own mini-Season.

The Season is something uniquely English. It cannot be defined. It is made of the summer, a number of 'events' and a frame of mind. It is this last – this frame of mind – that is not possible to pin down…

Football – Violent and Brutal

Say what you will, it is football that excites the country – but only when the Brits are winning. And football is not quite so genteel. Indeed, in its early days it was very rough. Playing it was forbidden by Edward II because of 'the great noise in the city caused by hustling over large balls.' Both Henry VIII and Elizabeth I enacted laws against this violent and brutal pastime. One author of the time described it as 'nothing but beastly fury and extreme violence…' Another said it was a 'develishe pastime' which led to 'brawling, murther, homicide, and great effusion of blood…'

A National Sporting Academy

Increasingly sporting success is equated with national success. It is amazing what sporting victories can do for morale. Is it patriotism?

Is it nationalism? Is it xenophobia? Perhaps it is all of these.

Remember the excitement when the English footballers – the no-hopers, the Hong Kong nightclubbers, the smashers of aeroplanes – after a dreary start, won some matches in Euro '96. Perhaps, just perhaps, they would go all the way and rekindle the spirit of the World Cup victory (how long ago was it?) 1966.

There was a similar buzz when, at Wimbledon, the young British hero, Tim Henman, raised the country's hopes with each of his victories.

Wow! What excitement! What anticipation!

Nobody really expected the English footballers to win the tournament, nor did they really expect that Mr Henman would come out on top. But there was hope. The country loves to win; or perhaps it loves the excitement of hoping to pull off something against very long odds.

There was even talk of an election – the national mood having swung to such an extent by the expectation – no, hope of victory – that Mr Major's side was said to have felt it had a fair chance of winning. And it went further. A plan was hatched to launch a great national sporting academy – a forcing-house for budding sportsmen and sportswomen, a training institution that would ensure the Brits could compete with the best in the world – and win! Shades of the old Eastern bloc.

Alas, we don't win.

A New International Game

Hang on! Didn't Britain teach the world about these sports. Shouldn't we be the best? *The Encyclopaedia Britannica* tells us that the game of Association Football is generally thought to be the outcome of the game of football as played at Cambridge University about the middle of the 19th century...

Having invented the game, Britain taught it to the world. There was a game between England and Scotland in November 1872; there was one between England and Wales in 1879 and one between England and Ireland in 1882. In 1896 amateur international matches were inaugurated with Germany, Austria and Bohemia...

The Old Lady suggests that we invent a new game. After all, for many years, we were tops at the games we exported to the rest of the world. If we invent and export a new international game – a game that we thought of; the rules of which we devised – we should, for a little while at least, be best at it. And win!

The rules need not be enormously complicated but they should be written in the sort of language that is peculiar to this country – the sort of English that foreigners just cannot fathom. Cricket is not played all over the world: it is played mainly in those countries that were once part of the British Empire, countries where English is spoken. This, we claim, is not because cricket is boring, nor because cricket is complicated. It is because the language of cricket is too difficult for foreigners...

Has anybody a really good idea for a new national (and international) sport? Why not send a set of rules to the new sporting academy? *The Old Lady* would be grateful for a copy…

Garth Hewitt was Editor of The Old Lady *from March 1996 until it closed in December 2007. This piece was published as the Editorial of the 303rd issue of* The Old Lady *dated September 1996.*

Reinventing the Sports Club

Pen Kent

In order to survive, the Sports Club has reinvented itself more than once — from a club for Bank members only to a more open club with members from the local community with no affiliation to the Bank. It is now available for hire for corporate entertainment and has leased part of the premises to the International Tennis Federation. It has also just leased nine acres to the Lawn Tennis Association to build the new national tennis centre. It has thus changed from an old fashioned club of people who worked together and played together to a much looser group of communities which have little to do with each other. Will this formula enable it to thrive for say the next 50 years? The History of the Club written to commemorate the 75th anniversary had a chapter called 'The Golden Years 1922-28'. Will there ever be another golden age for the Club at Roehampton?

During its history the Club has naturally reflected the social changes around it. It was founded in 1908 to promote the welfare of the staff – healthy minds in healthy bodies! The staff were then a small army of mainly male clerks living to the windward of the Big Smoke. For many of them the Club became a way of life, travelling after work at the Bank on Saturday morning to see and be seen as a player in an institution where promotion was slow and infrequent, and based on rather untesting criteria. Hence the Golden Years on the sports field. When I joined in 1961 – and played rugby after work on Saturday mornings – that tradition still lingered and some of the stalwarts of the 1920s and 30s were still about.

Of course the Bank of England was not the only employer of male, white collar workers to build sports clubs for the welfare of their staff in the affordable greenish belt on public commuter routes. The pattern of our away games was to visit the grounds of other banks, insurance companies and a few Old Boys clubs whose grounds were mainly acquired I guess at around the same period. That's the way we lived then.

But that was already changing when I arrived. The Clean Air Acts of 1956 and 1968 , and the shift (already started by the pressures of the Second World War) from male clerks to women clerks with keyboard skills to cope with the demands of IT moved the weight of staff catchment to the East in the lee of the once, but no longer Big Smoke. This made the location of the club convenient for fewer people.

So? Widen the appeal and make it more family-friendly – out went the male only bars and in came the swimming pool, toddlers pool and picnic area. Did you know the pool was deliberately made sub-competitive length to fend off the 'professionals'? Eligibility to play for Bank teams was opened initially to a small number of outsiders to keep the show on the road – and then to as many outsiders as it takes. For example the current 1st XV has no Bank players. The Bank staff has meanwhile continued to shrink from a peak of over 7000 in the 1970s to only just over 2000 now. Of the present 6000 Club members only 460 are current members of staff of the Bank. 800 are pensioners and 3500 are 'family' members with the majority related to pensioners. And career patterns have changed. When I joined, and for that matter for nearly the next 40 years, I answered the question, 'What do you do?' with, 'I work for the Bank of England'. Demonstrably a sense of belonging. But now? 'I am an economist/accountant/ lawyer/regulator'. Loyalty has shifted from the institution to the roles and the professions.

So? Widen the appeal (again)! And reduce the cost to the Bank by admitting more and more outsiders pursuing individual health activity and paying commercial rates – and lease even more of the grounds to the tennis world. The Club itself is now effectively an autonomous commercial concern, while the Bank continues to run the site.

Still the grounds are beautifully kept and of themselves suitable for professional levels of sport, like the pre-Wimbledon qualification tournament and the LTA Junior International Tournament. For many years the Club also provided training facilities for the national soccer and rugby sides and for Fulham FC but the rest of the facilities now lag behind the requirements of modern sport. So the shift has continued from a welfare club in its own right to a semi-commercial back-up facility for the Big Time. Not quite fair perhaps, but you know what I mean.

Pen Kent CBE was Executive Director of the Bank of England, 1994–97, having first joined the Bank in 1961. He was UK Alternate Director at the IMF, 1976–79. This article was first published in The Old Lady at Play *for the Threadneedle Club.*

CHAPTER TEN

The Old Lady at Sea

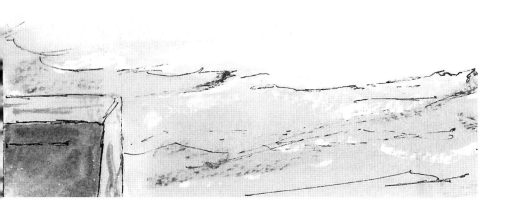

The Office Party

'We want just one more
for the musical chairs...'

'Goodness, Mr Hannington,
fifty-eight isn't old!'

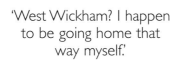

'West Wickham? I happen
to be going home that
way myself.'

'And how is the life
and soul of the party
this morning?'

The Old Lady at Sea

*I*n the first *Morning Rose*, an S&S 34, the Bank acquired in 1975 a boat with the unmistakable hallmark of first-class design and build. Every line marked her out as a thoroughbred.

In 1979 we took the old *Rose* down to Falmouth with a boatload of economists to visit the recently retired Chief of the Economic Intelligence Department, Michael Thornton MC in his new riverside home. Having arranged to meet him in his dinghy at St Mawes, we flew – to the mystification of the Coastguard and the Harbourmaster – the international signal:

E – I am directing my course to STARBOARD

I – I am directing my course to PORT

D – KEEP CLEAR – I am manoeuvring with
    difficulty

It was the nautical expression of a sentiment concerning economists shared by many: their model (or vessel) will take them anywhere, if only they know where they are and where they are going.

The 1979 Fastnet Race

A few weeks later in the Fastnet Race from Cowes to Plymouth via the Fastnet Rock off the Irish coast, *Morning Rose* gave us all a nasty fright. She was reported missing with no distress signal somewhere in the Western Approaches in extreme storm conditions. Many boats were lost or abandoned; 15 lives were lost and a major emergency rescue operation produced no news of the Bank boat. After three days we were all beginning to expect the worst, when, astonishingly, on the Thursday morning, she was identified approaching the Plymouth Breakwater.

Morning Rose had taken in a lot of water in rogue wave-conditions and had run off downwind with the electronics and radio out of action. This course took her the wrong side of Land's End and up the Bristol Channel. Only when the wind eased was she able to turn round and begin to beat her way back. The crew were intact, in good spirit and without injury, while the boat had proved herself to be an excellent sea-boat. I went down to bring her back from Plymouth to the Hamble, and then the following spring, on to London in St Katherine's Dock where the Governors could see for themselves the damage she had sustained.

The New Morning Rose

The new *Morning Rose*, an S&S SHE 36, acquired in 1980, was more suitable as a Club boat with a stronger engine and eight separate berths. One small incident sticks in the memory. We were entering Ormonville at half-tide with an eminent Fellow of the Royal Statistical Society and Yachtmaster cum laude as navigator. His precise chart-work could reduce our cocked-hat fixes to a single point and he seemed to know the 1200-page Nautical Almanac by heart.

Ormonville, at half-tide with a sea running is impressive. You gradually close the coast from the East. It is high, unbroken cliff, against which the breakers thunder. There is a mournful offshore buoy, a wreck and to seaward to the West, the jagged rocks of a long reef through which the strong Cotentin tide sluices and bursts with ferocity. In the narrow channel between the bank and the cliffs there was plenty of water for our seven-foot draft, although there are large drying rocks on either side.

Our navigator, having brought us meticulously to the leading marks, went below to call out the depth from the echo-sounder mounted above the navigator's table.

'Fifteen feet!', he called. There was no doubt about it. He had not noticed that the calibration had been switched to metres.

'Twelve, ten... nine!' a note of urgency had entered his voice.

'Seven!' – hysteria was almost discernible

'Six!' – a strangled cry – we would have been hard aground.

'Five, four!' – by which time in feet we could have paddled ashore.

Then a snort of understanding as we glided in sweetly up to the mooring.

First published in The Old Lady *in Spring 1992. Morning Rose II was followed by a succession of Bank of England yachts, each called Ingotism, the last of which was sold in late 2006.*

Editor's note

My interest in offshore sailing dated from the day I joined the Bank of England in 1959. I was greeted by the Principal of the Staff Office with what I had begun to recognise as a familiar gambit:

'I see you're not much of a sportsman. What do you mean Light Fell-walking and Sailing Fireflies at Port Meadow? You should try something bigger!'

AC Sandison, I later discovered, had made his name among the Class 1 owners of the Royal Ocean Racing Club by offering his services as a gourmet chef in return for a promise that he could always wear his carpet slippers – and therefore never have to go on deck. He was prone to waken the new watch with a steaming mug of tea and his own guttural rendering of 'Jesus wants me for a sunbeam'.

He sent me off to Lieutenant-Commander Alan Paul, Secretary of the RORC, who promptly despatched me on an Easter cruise round the Channel Islands followed by a trip to Belle Ile and the Morbihan. Next I took a call from him in the Bank asking if I could sail as Navigator on the Club boat, Griffin II, in the race from Plymouth to St Nazaire. I pointed out that I had no qualifications or formal training in navigation, to which he replied: 'Now's your chance to learn'.

More by luck than by good judgement, we came second to Zulu navigated by Francis Chichester with Adlard Coles in third place. By then I had completed the minimum number of racing miles for ordinary RORC membership which I enjoyed happily for the next 45 years.

The Verse of Jeremy Morse

He That Knows

He that knows not and knows not that he knows not,
Shun him for he is a fool.
He that knows not and knows that he knows not,
Teach him for he will learn.

He that knows and knows not that he knows,
Wake him for he is asleep.
He that knows and knows that he knows,
Follow him for he is wise.

Quoting a Persian proverb taught him at age 9 by his schoolmaster in
1937, and which he has always remembered.

1-10
Numberless son,
Let me teach you
(Or you teach me)
Your natural lore.
While we're alive
Arithmetic's
One way to heaven
An infinite, straight
And narrow line
To guide all men

The Old Lady, 1965

CHAPTER ELEVEN

The Library Centenary Award 1950–1990

Music and Dance at the Bank

Suppose the great strong room one night,
Were entered by a fairy,
With magic wand, and flashing light,
And garments few and airy.

Suppose the money bags came out
And danced a minuetto;
Suppose the scales then joined the rout
And sang un gran duetto.

Suppose Monseignor Gold laid by
His case cum dignitate
And stuck his eyeglass in his eye,
And called for lobster pâté.

Suppose my Lady Silver smiled
On Lord Fitz-Bronze the night long
And threepenny pieces all ran wild
And hoped they'd all keep bright long.

Suppose a shovel and a weight
Were telling tara-diddles;
Suppose the notes walked out sedate,
And asked each other riddles.

Suppose the keys forgot their place,
And danced a double-shuffle:
Suppose the half-pence ran a race
And tried the notes to ruffle.

Suppose the wine was good and strong:
Suppose the talk was witty
And, before it gets too long,
Suppose – I end my ditty.

Our (Bank of England) Magazine 1884

150

The Library Centenary Awards 1950 – 1990

To mark the centenary of the Bank of England Library in 1950, an annual award was established for the best contribution to *The Old Lady* in the previous year. A prominent personality from the world of letters was invited to judge all the material in the four quarterly issues and to present the award at an annual dinner. The report of each Judge was announced and published each year in *The Old Lady* and many of the reports became interesting and witty literary pieces in their own right.

The choice of one single person each year – and not a committee – is very much in line with the Bank's traditional way of doing things. You define carefully what it is you want done. You choose the best person available and then leave him or her to get on with the job. You expect them to carry out the instructions carefully and you give them wherever they are whatever support they ask for but you do not interfere. They, in their turn, know that they have – with due discretion – to come up with the right result.

The list of the Judges is quite remarkable. As Joan Bakewell put it in reply to the final invitation in 1990:

'The list of your past judges offers as temptation enough the prospect of adding one's name to such a list.'

Reading all the reports in sequence, I am sure that none of the Judges bothered to look what their predecessors had concluded. Nonetheless, there are some common themes: an astonishment at the variety of the material; the difficulty of choosing between a wealth of good prose and verse, the need to give credit to lively

151

sports commentaries, copious book, theatre and film reviews and much other material. Also the Judges had to take account of well-researched interviews with and articles about the leading personalities connected with the Bank, some of historic significance, speeches by the Governors and lively commentaries on the economic issues of the day.

The way out of this dilemma of choice for many of the Judges was to identify everything which they considered first-class: in total over 300 other contributors were named in their reports and given high credit. These accolades reinforced morale markedly, spurring the Editor and contributors to new effort and the Editorial Committee to rigour in eliminating self-serving rubbish and absolutely anything with the slightest whiff of scandal or intrigue, while at the production stage, nothing but near-perfect English, punctuation, spelling and proof-reading was acceptable.

Many Judges pointed out that writing under these constraints by amateurs, some seeing themselves in print for the first time, could not hope to meet professional standards. Nonetheless, most of the Judges recognised that the sum of the whole had a special character of its own – a product of high and enduring quality and endeavour. Laurie Lee, put it well in 1977:

> *'Through* The Old Lady, *the Bank of England speaks with a refreshing variety of tongues... These packed pages show expanding ripples of personality and imagination, at times eccentric, scholarly or hearty; expressed in poems and prose of widely different quality but combining to speak for a balanced society'.*

For Claire Tomalin (1977) the fascination is of insights into an otherwise closed society:

'... that's what strikes the outsider peeping in through the pages of The Old Lady... a series of hives buzzing with particular enthusiasms and skills'

Paul Theroux (1981) concluded along the same lines:

'It is never less than pleasurable to enter a world in which people are writing about the things which interest them. The Old Lady is one such world.'

LP Hartley (1958) speaks of finding everywhere;

'the self-discipline of the professional's and the spontaneity of the amateur's touch – a rare combination.'

Joan Bakewell (1990) spotted an essential of the Bank way of saying things:

'The form is a taut one: style and content fused in the moment to say one thing worth saying and then stop. I am impressed how again and again the pages of your magazine provide just that'.

Marghanita Laski (1980) chose two pieces by John Deacon as the most impressive as they focussed on craftsmen in relation to their work for the Bank:

'Both are absorbing to anyone interested in craftwork in general'

Katherine Whitehorn (1983) was astonished to discover that *The Old Lady* was not only readable but amusing:

'When my husband saw your publication on the table, he didn't know what I was up to – a common condition with husbands, especially if they are writers; and he thought it was a regular women's magazine with a remarkably inept title: who's ever going to buy that ...

153

I'm indeed sorry to confess that we hadn't heard about you before, and the more so as you just about saved our lives over the Whit bank holiday. It was the wettest Whitsun for forty years, we spent it on a small boat, and during the nineteen hours when we were shut up in the cabin, we actnally laughed aloud reading The Old Lady.'

The collection of the 42 winning entries (6 women and 36 men) and the comments of the 41 Judges (6 women and 35 men), suitably edited, would itself make an entertaining book of some literary merit and interest, given the distinction and eloquence of the Judges and the fact that they had all been set the same difficult task.

To convey something of the character of the various anecdotes included in the Judges' reports, I conclude with:

Brian Johnston, broadcaster, opened his report in 1984 with:

I was particularly pleased when I received a letter from Roger Woodley asking me first to judge and then to come and present the Library Centenary Award. I was so pleased, in fact, that I rang him up the same afternoon at the Bank of England and asked to speak to him, and his secretary said: 'Well, actually, he's not here this afternoon.' So I said: 'Oh, doesn't he work in the afternoon?' and she said: 'No, it's the mornings that he doesn't work – he doesn't come in in the afternoons'.

Ned Sherin opened his report for 1989 with:

'At one stage of the Second World War, General Sikorski, the leader of the exiled Polish Government tried vainly to raise a loan in the City to support his forces. Finally he approached Churchill to use his influence with the bankers. They spoke in French. Churchill shook his head sadly, 'Non, mon Général, quand je suis avec les Vieux Dames de Threadneedle Street, je suis impotent.'

154

Judges and Winners of the Centenary Award

	Judge	Winner
1950	Sir Osbert Sitwell	HA Venting Gibbs
1951	Compton Mackenzie	Richard Powers
1952	Raymond Mortimer	Joan Bridges
1953	John Betjeman	Frank Dancaster
1954	Sir Harold Nicholson	Peter Noble
1955	Lord David Cecil	AS Cope
1956	Andre Maurois	Leslie Bonnet
1957	JB Priestley	Brian Ash
1958	LP Hartley	DJH Chetwin
1959	VS Pritchett	Leslie Bonnet
1960	Stephen Spender	Joan Bridges
1961	John Lehmann	Christopher Elston
1962	John Freeman	Stanley Cerely
1963	Victor Gollancz	Leslie Bonnet
1964	Leslie Bonnet	Basil Hone
1965	Cecil Harmsworth King	Frank Daly
1966	Pamela Hansford Johnson	Joan Bridges
1967	William Luscombe	Frank Daly
1968	HE Bates	Joan Bridges
1969	Lord Francis-Williams	William Maclaine and Christine Coldicott
1970	Sir Robert Lusty	Stanley Cerely
1971	Bernard Levin	David Nye
1972	John Fowles	David Pollard
1973	John Arlott	JCM Webb
1974	Antonia Fraser	Roger Woodley
1975	Brian W Aldiss	FR Levander

1976	Claire Tomalin	John Alves
1977	Laurie Lee	Stanley Cerely
1978	Peter Ustinov	Jacqueline Pearce
1979	William Rees-Mogg	Roger Woodley
1980	Marghanita Laski	John Deacon
1981	Paul Theroux	Pamela Clayton
1982	Philip Howard	Derrick Byatt
1983	Katherine Whitehorn	Roger Barnes
1984	Brian Johnston	Fred Seagreave
1985	Peter Porter	Jane Collier
1986	John Mortimer	Martin Russell
1987	Frank Delaney	Bryan Brown
1988	Robert Robinson	Jasper Rootham
1989	Ned Sherrin	Ian McQuire

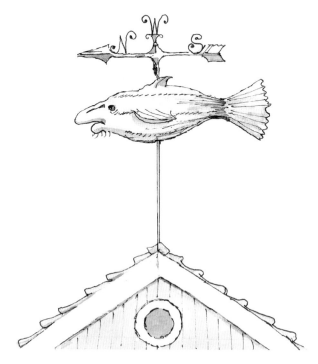

Design for the sturgeon wind-vane at the Sports Club, Roehampton.

Notes Great and Small

One day a mad musician came
Inside the Bank's great portals.
He was a man with famous name,
And one of Art's Immortals.

He brought a cheque and asked for gold,
And then was most politely told:
'Notes great and small are used by all,
By even Art's Immortals.

'The only notes for which I've use
Are minim, crochet, quaver;
I will not take your lame excuse
I don't like your behaviour.'

'The sort of notes I know,' said he
'Are those which make sweet harmony:
Breve, semibreve I will receive
And minim, crochet, quaver.'

The cashier spoke in accents grave
Andante sostenuto
'Our notes are like those on the stave;
I'll make this clear to you, so.

'When Trade is very good, you know,
Notes may be spent prestissimo;
When times are bad, and very sad,
Notes should be ritenuto.'

J H McNulty, An Imaginary Visit to the Bank, 1930

'Do you have anything for a static Assistant Principal?'

CHAPTER TWELVE

The Old Lady of
Threadneedle Street
(1921–2007)

'I Have a Mobile, a Cordless, E-mail and Fax'

I have a mobile, a cordless, e-mail and fax,
I must be in touch, I never can relax.
I'm a tycoon in media, have the use of a plane,
Today I'm in Sweden, tomorrow in Spain.
My wife's a high flier, she directs TV
She's very agreesive competing with me.
We view with each other, Who's under most stress?

Things will be different, starting this morning.
I'll get rid of the e-mail, to hell with the fax,
I will learn to play bridge and I'll start to relax,
I will go for long walks, start smelling the flowers
And will really appreciate all the long hours.
I can look forward to re-modelling my life –
Let's hope I can also re-model the wife!

Michael Carter, The Dangers of Stress, 1999

The Old Lady of
Threadneedle Street
(1921–2007)

*T*he Old Lady has by no means been the only staff magazine in the Bank of England. *The Bank of England Journal* flourished between 1808 and 1810, *The Black Cat* in 1860 and *Our Magazine* 1884-5 and others in the pre-World War One years included *Bank Notes*, *The Advance* and, at the Liverpool Branch, *The Bank Messenger*.

In June 1919, almost two years before *The Old Lady* was finally launched, *The Britannia Quarterly* appeared as a 'downstairs' rival to the 'upstairs' *Old Lady*. Its earthy humour and bright, breezy style (see pages 119-120) made it consistently, quarter by quarter, more readable. *The Britannia Quarterly* lasted 74 years until July 1993.

In 1924 *Horizon*, described in Bank documents as 'outrageous', was terminated after four issues by co-opting two of its founders onto *The Old Lady* publications committee. In 1930-31 *Outburst* survived ten manuscript, two cyclostyled and two printed issues before they were declared subversive and after the Editor had left the Bank. It was then decided that there should be a regular two-to-four-page outlet for anonymous protest: *Flyleaf* has appeared as a prominent separate feature in every issue of *The Old Lady* from 1932 until the last in December 2007.

A Complete Set

*L*ike so many others in the Bank of England, my first awareness of *The Old Lady* quarterly magazine dates from the Parlours Waiting Room prior to being interviewed by the Staff Director and Bank selection panel. I remember thinking at the time (1958) what an extraordinary document this was with its deadly title, drab cover and thick antique paper, not to mention its ponderous style, endless sports reports and lengthy obituaries. Only later did I realise how misleading first impressions can be.

It did not cross my mind to contribute to *The Old Lady* until 1962. I had purchased for £145 late one night in a pub in Falmouth a 50-60-year old Mevagissey oyster smack and had asked two contemporaries in Overseas Office (Malcolm Gill and Anthony Houchen) to help me sail it back to Poole. As a mark of thanks and apology for the lack of engine, limited food and water and miserable accommodation, I sent in a short text with sketches of us under full topsail and flying jib and staysail and fully reefed in a squall. To my surprise, the Governor, the Earl of Cromer, sent for me to say how much he had enjoyed the article. 'I have a boat...', he went on, the first of many such conversations, although the boat he was referring to turned out to be a large motor-yacht with professional crew based in Cannes.

In 1970 I had another stroke of luck. Michael Williams, the Editor of *The Old Lady* rang to say that a Bank widow wanted to get rid of the first fifty bound annual volumes of the magazine and would I be interested in having them. There was, as I soon discovered, a hidden agenda to his proposal. I collected them the following weekend and installed them on two shelves at our fireside where they remain today. The 37 subsequent volumes, in their blue and gold Old Lady bindings live in a bookcase at our bedside.

Only when I began to plough my way steadily through their (now 20,800) pages did I realise that I had been handed the 'Holy Grail' of the Bank of England. Here, at my fingertips was a complete record of almost everything of interest that had happened in the Bank since 1920. A band of enthusiastic amateurs from the staff had unearthed endless stories going right back to the foundation of the Bank and they all published their findings in its pages – a treasure-trove indeed. For the editor, whose skills of delegation were such that he simultaneously edited a couple of horse-racing magazines and was only rarely to be found in the Bank after mid-day, I could reliably supply, from the apppointment, retirement and obituary lists and notices published each quarter, full details of anyone in or retired from the Bank, or deceased, and often a lot of other relevant material.

For many of us posted abruptly overseas in remote deserts, jungles and isolated islands and even those condemned for long periods to the cocktail circuits of Washington, Tokyo, Moscow, Paris and Basel, an occasional contribution to *The Old Lady* provided a convenient and polite means of reminding the Governors and others that one was still out there and might require further employment on return.

As I ploughed my way through *The Old Ladies* I flagged up everything of interest and gradually distilled the best into new articles on the various Offices of the Bank, which were published in *The Old Lady* under the description 'The Wild Thyme Manuscript' and in a series of annual 36-page booklets published for the Threadneedle Club.

In the 250th issue in July 1983, my first History of The Old Lady was published together with my offer to sell my complete set for £5000 to provide generous literary prizes and incentives for young writers. Fortunately there were no takers, but the Governors responded by providing the £5000 and announcing the new arrangements, so sadly entitled the David and Susan Nye Memorial Awards (see page 178), in the next issue in September 1983.

The Spirit of the Bank of England

Journal, 1808

On the appointment of Mr Hase to succeed the late Mr Abraham Newland* as Chief Cashier of the Bank of England

Ye Directors of England's vast treasure,
In *Darkness* why always exist?
When Abraham Newland departed,
In the Bank he was certainly *Mist*.
Still a *Cloud* overhangs your proceedings;
I see it, I own with amaze!
(Though perhaps you make
Light of the matter),
He now is succeeded by *Haze*!

*Abraham Newland was born on 23.4.1730 and was elected to the Service of the Bank on 25.2.1748. He resigned in 1807 after 59 years service. During his 29 years (1778-1807) as the Chief Cashier, he never slept a single night outside the Bank.

The Perils of Contributing to the Bank Magazine 1884

On Seeing My First Poem in Print (Anon) published in Our (Bank of England) Magazine

Ah! Here it is! I'm famous now!
An author and a poet
It really is in print – ye gods
How proud I'll be to show it.

Why bless my soul – here's something strange!
What can the paper mean
By talking of the graceful brooks
'That gander oe'r the green'..

'Hast thou no tears?' The T's left out;
'Hast thou no ears' instead
'I hope that thou art dear' is put
'I hope that thou art dead'.

Whoever saw in such a space
So many blunders crammed?
'Those gentle eyes bedimmed' is spelt
'Those gentle eyes be damned'.

Oh Fame! Thou cheat of human bliss
Why did I ever write?
I wish my poem had been burnt.
Before it saw the light.

The Twenties

The continuity of *The Old Lady* has very deep roots. Everyone in the twenties seemed to have recognised the need to document the handsome doomed buildings, to salvage and catalogue the furniture and records, to publicise all the Roman and medieval artefacts which began to appear from the foundations and to explain the sumptuous design and adornment of the new building. The archive included people. As the editors put it:

> 'It seems incredible that an ancient institution like our own should have no domestic history, that men in thousands should have come and gone these 200 years and left no trace, lived out their lives within these walls and vanished...in their ranks, perhaps, were poets and artists, scholars and wise men... there must have been 'perfect clerks' and very imperfect, rogues and honest men, roisterers and braggarts and dare-devils, as well as quiet and peaceable folk. A very motley crew, my masters. Yet they have bequeathed naught to us.'

The Thirties – The Golden Age

Ten Outstanding Contributors in the Thirties

Allan Fea	Bank Memories of 1880–1890
W Marston Acres	Bank Governors (long series)
W Marston Acres	Criminal Trials re the Bank (long series)
'Shamayim'	Love among the Ledgers

Stephen Chant	The Chronicle of Wasted Time
RPW	Sic Transit! I come to bury 5% War
Richard Powers	Jaunts and Jollities (long series)
Hermann Willke	The Nazi Impact on the Reichsbank
WE Lefler	Old Times in the Bank (long series)
Andrew Bonella	The Isle of Dogs (a tall short story)

The Editors of The Old Lady

Epitaph for the Editor of The Old Lady

They hanged him today, I hear
That's good! The time was ripe
He killed *The Old Lady*, or pretty near,
By filling her up with tripe.

The Old Lady, September 1933

1921–1929	*Edited by Committee or Joint Editorial Panel*
1929–1930	RJ Hastings
1930–1934	JA Giuseppi
1934–1935	Stephen Chant
1936–1939	Leslie Bonnet
1939–1946	Beryl Langford*
1946–1952	Richard Powers
1952–1960	Frank Dancaster
1960–1971	Michael Williams
1972–1974	Frank Daly
1974–1977	Llewellyn Sutton
1977–1983	David Nye
1983–1989	David Pollard
1989–1995	Steven Young
1996 –2007	Garth Hewitt

*Jointly with JA Giuseppi from September 1939 to September 1940

The Product of Human Beings

'The Old Lady *does not emerge from a computerised programme nor is it subject to the contemporary tyranny of management and financial terminology.* The Old Lady *is mercifully the product of human beings*'

Sir Robert Lusty, Judge of the Annual Library Award, 1970

Three Old Lady Poets

Jasper Rootham

The Shining Stream of Language

There is something about diamonds –
Not just a girl's best friend
('Diamond Hard' as a Bank Director
once said of a tycoon
with whom, in the public interest,
he had had a clash of heads.)

Then there was Queen Victoria
who was given whopping diamonds
on her Diamond Jubilee.
She was a very old lady, but younger still by far
than the one who sits in Threadneedle Street
and used to show her head
on the sovereigns I once handled
as a boy, so long ago,

168

in days when (you must believe it)
I could plonk one on the counter
against two pounds of cod
and get the change in silver
as bright as the fishes' scales.

Diamonds go on, and so does gold
But both of them are dumb
and it is surely, is it not,
words which illumine all
our wisdoms and our follies?

And so it is a pleasure to salute
a different Old Lady
who at sixty years old
today still uses the shining stream of language
(the deepest river of all)
which helps contemporary Ms and Mister
to respond to an ancient call.

From The Old Lady's Diamond Jubilee, *1981*

Jasper St J Rootham entered the Service on 20th May 1946 and was pensioned as Chief of Overseas Department on 1st August 1967. He died in 1990. He contributed frequently to The Old Lady *in prose and verse. Chatto & Windus published two volumes of prose,* Miss-Fire *and* Demi-Paradise, *in 1946 and 1960. His* Collected Verses *1928-1972 appeared in 1973 and there were four more volumes of verse before the publication of his 5000-line autobiography in verse,* Affirmation, *in 1982. The following extract is taken from his Retirement Notice published in* The Old Lady *in 1967.*

Jasper St John Rootham

Chief of Overseas

Retirement Notice

'From Tonbridge, he proceeded to the college of his name at Cambridge where he obtained a first in Classics and then joined the Civil Service. Advancement there was rapid, and in a relatively short period of time he had progressed into the Prime Minister's office. Shortly after Munich, the then Prime Minister walked, at the end of one very long day, into the private secretaries' room only to find Jasper standing on his head, illustrating to the other three secretaries how easily it could be done.

'Came the War, when he quit the Treasury to take up his Territorial Army commitments, flatly refusing to be reserved. He was in Yugoslavia with Mihailovic, when the latter was ditched by the Allies (so, oddly enough, was Ruper Raw); ultimately he reached Italy in an American plane which, on landing, was found to be carrying a small peach tree on the undercarriage, uprooted on a dicey takeoff.

'In his spare time, he farms on the borders of Cambridgeshire, writes poetry and prose, is on the General Advisory Council of the BBC as well as being, first and foremost, an enthusiastic family man.'

Orpheus in the Underground

Frank Dancaster

The Central Line

Westwards he rides, with little ease,
One of a swaying load
Bound from St Paul's to Marble Arch
Along the lower road.

Another, by the higher road,
Mid slime and jolting stone,
Rides westward, too, with no more ease
Upon a sledge, alone

Nor knows an unborn man, beneath,
Prays for his soul, as he
Journeys from Newgate's frowning wall
To Tyburn's bloody tree.

Frank Dancaster, 1955, editor of The Old Lady, *1952-60*

'Cast that Balance Up'

David Nye

Although the wind's direction's changed
      The traffic's noise is only distant still
An early Cuckoo and the pigeon's purr
      And a bright miscellany of song
            Are what you hear ...

And if you've lost the sense of these
      Stand still and think awhile
Of what you've gained and what is gone
      And cast that balance up,
            There's where you are.

The Sense of Spring, June 1968

Only Half the Sum

Yesterday when I saw the moon
Tired and blurry-eyed,
And you were not beside me,
I realised that everything
Without you
Was only half the sum.

No Man's an Island, September 1968

Three Old Lady Editors

Frank Dancaster

Time Does not Stand Still

Frank Dancaster was Editor of The Old Lady *from 1952 to 1960. This eloquent and profound letter from Damascus was written on active military service in the Middle East in the middle of the second world war and published under the heading 'The Laurels All Are Cut' in the September 1943 issue of* The Old Lady.

> 'Nous n'irons plus aux bois,
> Les lauriers sont coupés.'

I sat one evening in a café in Damascus, drinking claret and listening politics. For I am one of the irresponsibles who, at any rate so far, have never found the enthusiasm to talk politics and have found considerable difficulty, with patience, to listen politically. However all that is changed, changed utterly. A terrible duty is born.

172

The soldier who was speaking, and I, had fallen into talk, drawn together by our common race and tongue in the midst of the human jungle which is Damascus, the town where Armageddon is in the faces of those who pass you by. Outside, the intolerable clangour of a damascene evening flowered with the darkness. Tram bells jangled with frenzied iteration; shrill cries gashed the tepid air; motor cars honked like enraged beasts and an interminable shuffling of bare, booted, sandaled and slippered feet rose through it all like a dust of sound.

The conversation started, as all conversations do between soldiers in the East, with savage and obscene reflections on the manners and customs of the Orient. And then on to war. And then on to the causes of war and then on to the system, the bad old system, which had allowed 1939 to occur so soon after 1914. 'This time we've really got to alter all that', said the soldier and he was a man convinced. There was no disagreeing with what he said...

This Illusion of Permanence
The hardest thing to comprehend emotionally when you are first abroad at war is the simple fact that time does not stand still. The day on which you leave your country is carved in deep relief on the façade of time. You do not know where you are going; you are not certain of getting there; you may never come back. You feel that temporarily, and possibly permanently, everything has come to an end. You look your last on all things lovely. There, across the harbour waters, is England and the life you have known. Look at it, cram into those last agonising moments all that you can of English faces and voices and streets...

But as time passes and one year imperceptibly becomes two and you grow older by those insensible degrees, which are none the less real because you do not feel them yourself nor are those in daily contact with you aware of them, this illusion of permanence, that time will stand still, is slowly but relentlessly undermined…

You become vaguely disquieted though precisely why, or by what, you cannot say because the whole trend of your mind is trying to thwart the apprehension of a fact that will, once fully grasped, hurt and wound you. But you cannot play Canute with time. Those waves are of a sea whose primal force lies beyond the uncounted millions of souls it has drowned. The realisation has to be accepted that the people and places you know are changing; the pattern shifting; the very texture being renewed.

A Promise has been Broken
Your letters are starred with death, with names that mean nothing to you, with relationships you had not foreseen, reactions for which you had not allowed and, perhaps the most stunning blow of all, with births, the emergence of a new generation. Before the biological fact of nine months the immobility of time is no longer a tenable illusion. You have clutched at time and it has crumbled in your hands like brittle chalk. Something cold touches you lightly and passes on, a gust of wind which ruffles the water and then all is still. But there lingers in your mind the shadow of an idea of treachery, as though it was life itself which had betrayed you. But this, you feel, is, and yet cannot be, must not, at all costs, be. This is change, and absurdly you feel that somehow, somewhere, a promise has been broken, a pledge unfulfilled…

There has been a cataclysmic dynamiting of the wall of illusion and not of my illusion only but of that of thousands, and we were looking over the rubble at alien and rather terrifying landscapes, at unfamiliar roads down which strangers walked, at a house here and a factory there, and new fashions in hats and ideas.

Preaching the Gospel of Tomorrow

So I began to understand the conflict in my mind as I sat drinking claret in that Damascus café and listened to the soldier talking. He was doubly right. Things would have to be different and there was little doubt this time that they would be. And he was young enough to accept the implications, whereas I, sipping my wine and with a spring of intolerable sadness welling up within me, knew that I was not any longer young enough.

For whenever there occurs one of those violent paroxysms of humanity, a war or pestilence sufficiently enormous to sever the generations within a decade, to cause a fissure, a sudden sharp faulting of life, then when the rumbling and dust have subsided, of necessity many must find themselves on the wrong side of the chasm...And I knew, while the thoughts slipped across my mind, as a shadow slips across a cornfield, that I should be on the wrong side of the unbridgeable, uncrossable chasm.

And so I said nothing because a sense of failure and cowardice restrained me and the fear of being identified with the old muddle and greed and injustice. He was preaching the gospel of tomorrow, of justice and equity and decent living, and I sat there looking into the deep reds of my glass and muttering, *'Nous n'irons plus aux bois.'*

The Tree is Beautiful

Outside was Damascus, filthy, strident, the oldest inhabited city in the world. That too would change, but slowly, as things were meant to change, not by a sudden, violent shock that twisted the girders of a man's life and left him the alternative of living on the slant or of courageously and ruthlessly tearing down the structure and starting again.

It was an alternative which did not exist for me or for my kind. My mind was full of knick-knacks, of no more use, no longer in the fashion or the mood, but which I would never have the heart to jettison. How can you be expected suddenly to throw away all the pretty gilt-edged ideas which have stood on the shelves of your mind for so long?...

We were not built to withstand the stress of Time moving flat-out. Living things grow slowly. For generations, the tree is beautiful and the seasons cannot be hurried from their rhythm. If man's life is short, using the tape measure of eternity; if it is brief, a tick of the second-hand of eternity's clock, it is also, in its own background in its intended setting, long.It is a growth, a progression, not a series of frenzied jerks and muscular twitchings.

'You'll see', he ended confidently, 'they'll alter it all this time.' It was true, or at least, I did not doubt that they would try to. It was all altered already, not yet wisely and constructively, but perhaps that would come. I did not know and, shamefully, I did not care.

'*Les lauriers sont coupés,*' I muttered and walked out into the tepid evening.

Retrospect and Anticipation

Beryl Langford

As we go to press, England has been at war with Germany for practically a year. During these twelve months we have learned to think calmly of prospects which a few years ago might have brought us panic, for we have the calm of preparedness and a just cause. The radio and the newspapers give us some amount of daily news, the Prime Minister [Winston Churchill] sums up, from time to time, the broader, national aspects of the war. Compared with these matters it may seem trivial to ask ouselves what has been the effect of the past twelve months upon *The Old Lady*. And yet this is our private journal and in its pages and in its progress in the affections of the Bank we may trace to some extent the effect of the war on our individual lives.

We want to see the circulation of the magazine going up. Above all , when these unhappy war days are over, we want to be able to look back at *The Old Lady* and find a truer record of our trials and difficulties, our amusements, our literary and artistic efforts, of our work and of our play.

Beryl Langford edited The Old Lady *from 1939 to 1946 with help from J A Guiseppi in the first year.*

Editorial for the 250th Issue of The Old Lady 1 July 1983

David Nye

The death of a relation, one dearly loved, focuses the thoughts on the inescapable movement forward of life. Such a sorrow forces home the realisation that our existence allows no escape from change, from the unexpected, from the whole range of life's possibilities, from comedy to deepest tragedy. Experience dispels what one might call the Blandings Castle illusion, that perpetual Shropshire summer is humanly attainable. For even as the mallet swings and the croquet ball glides through the hoop into a patch of evening sunlight, in the midst of such domestic peace, time opens the crevasse at our feet.

We none of us know, however secure behind the love of those around us, or bolstered by power and possessions, what even the next moment may mean to us. To imagine otherwise is to be at the very least, unprepared...

Looking back through two hundred and fifty issues of this magazine one gains one impression that might help us to have an inkling of our fate. Making adjustment for the major outside influences such as war, life for Bank staff has never been either endlessly gloomy nor continuously rich and splendid. Our little pendulum, like all the others, swings to and fro. If it goes too far one way, then, to everyone's amazement, against all predictions, staff will start leaving; too far the other and some killjoy will step in. (Of course, even to point out something so obvious risks being proved wrong tomorrow.)

It is remarkable how very like we are to the imaginative people who launched *The Old Lady* in 1921 and who wrote in it then and in succeeding years. Their life, and so in all probability ours also, moved between periods of rich and lean; but it was always changing.

They tell us that much, and a great deal else, in what they left behind in words and pictures, humour and poetry, in this unimportant little domestic organ - which has drawn out so much effort, talent, even love, from Bank staff, to arrive safely at this landmark of 250 editions, in excellent heart for the invisible future.

Two weeks later, on 16 July 1983, David Nye, together with his wife and three young daughters, perished in a helicopter accident between Penzance and the Scillies.

'I Know a Bank'

I know a bank where peaceful rest
Beneath the laurel and by roses blessed
Who play the game to their own rules
The heirs of England's sporting best

Britannia, umpire, keeps the score
Defends the wicket, hears the shout
By raised right hand she indicates
Those who are in and who's now out.

There is a music in the air
Glimpses of notes, a flash of gold
The clink of silver coin, and horns
The athletes together turn their heads

Like skittles in serried rank they come
Wth cheers and song, a merry band
In search of Olympian fair play
In England's green and copper land.

From Understanding the Bank Façade, *by Paul Tempest*
The Flyleaf Rejects File, May 1995

Extracts from Flyleaf (1932–2007)

March 1933 – A fine long leg
During the recent controversy over body-bowling tactics, a Clerk immersed in a newspaper article on the technicalities of the subject, astonished the tea-table by asking: 'Can anyone tell me the difference between a fine long leg and a silly mid-on?'

There was a pained silence. Then I told him all I knew and left him to find out what a silly mid-on is.

March 1943 – A cross-section from the bar
The discussion was getting well on the way and it was a good hour after the time we had all promised to be home. 'Now,' said someone, 'we'll take a cross-section...'

'That reminds me – I must be off' said someone else, 'I suppose you are talking about our wives.'

March 1953 – Prelude to Toasting a Bank Victory
'Drinking before driving is putting the quart before the hearse.'

March 1963 – Annual Leave
'Hope he enjoyed his leave as much as we did.'

March 1973 – Information for Bank Tourists
1. An ancient right of way entitles pedestrians to use the path across the Garden Court. When you reach the far side, knock on one of the windows and an employee will be happy to escort you through to the Bullion Yard.

2. Every Thursday the Chief Cashier stands in the Front Hall holding his official staff of office and greets visitors to the Bank. You will recognise him by his tricorn hat.

3. The famous Old Lady of Threadneedle Street is, in fact, still alive and presides over tea every afternoon at 3.00 pm. Buy a ticket on the 5th Floor.

March 1983 – A Very Dangerous Christmas Tree

Dear Frost

One very jolly innovation this year was a Christmas Tree in the Front Hall. You can imagine that the very decent sized tree was a mere cone when the first committee was set up to consider the wheeze. Apart from the horrendous cost of the lights, the Health and Safety dangers of people walking into it after lunch, the Security Force screening the parcels and the problem of finding a willing fairy in the Bank, there was then the cost of sweeping up the needles…

Yours in limbo

George

March 1993 – A Whiter Shade of Pale

We have been deluged with complaints about the new £10 note…cricket enthusiasts from all over the home counties have complained that the colours are so weak it is impossible to see where the creases are on the cricket pitch. In future the colours will be much more daring, but in order to frustrate unscrupulous people with colour photocopiers, the back of the note will now be in black and white.

March 2003 – The Feast of the Passover

Dear Frost,

I've been on one of those courses that shows you how to look on the bright side; always seeing a half-full glass rather than a half-empty one; and how to generally upset all those around you with irrepressible bonhomie. I have to say it works a treat. As you well remember, Frostie, the Bank is full of glum dismal-Jimmies in February on account of the St Valentine's Day massacre or Feast of the Passover or however else you want to describe the distribution of the annual bonuses… Quoting our great war-time leader, I assured Norman that never, in the field of office conflict, had so few deprived so many of so much.

Yours in ebriation

George

1934 – XXX

Why not drink in litres? My diary says that one litre equals 1.76 pints. It also says, 'To convert litre to pint multiply by 50 and divide by 88'. A better way would be to drink a part of each litre.

1944 – Materfamilias

'I always say it doesn't matter how much noise they make so long as it keeps them quiet.'

1954 – Shorts from reports

- A model clerk, but not a working model.

- Would make a good schoolmistress, if she knew anything.

- Is always sitting about wrapped in thwart.

1964 – Flyleaf's mediocre food guide

The Bu Hao Fan lies in one of the murkier alleyways off Dean Street and owes most of its success to the determination of its owner, Mr Foo, to keep later hours than his occidental competitors, thereby pulling in the greater part of the after-eleven trade. This consists, in the main, of strangers to the West End, usually provincials and foreigners who, after being ejected from the neighbouring public houses, are either too hungry or too intoxicated to care what they eat.

1974 – Art show preview

The exhibits seem to be about as awful as last year's but the wine is a little better.

1984 – The new enhanced increment slip

Dear Frost

Black Thursdays aren't what they used to be in generating passion and hysteria, but this year's was awaited with special eagerness because the Bank was unveiling its new 'enhanced' increment slip – the slip is the piece of paper which, for egalitarian purposes, we all get now, whether the increment is real or imaginary, and which replaced the serried ranks of the former Chiefs of Establishments who, in your time, used to come into their own for half a day distributing the Bank's equivalent of Maundy Money. Unfortunately the eagerness quickly evaporated when it was discovered that it was the slip that was enhanced, not the increment.

Yours expectantly,
George

1994 – Limited opportunities

Dear Frost

Last time's moan about Unequal Opportunities has paid off handsomely. The Bank has agreed that I can have time off in lieu of pre-menstrual tension in addition to my paternity leave. So what with that, my half day a week study leave, two weeks sick leave, five weeks GL, 12 days flexi, 4 days special leave to recover from the Tercentenary Knees-up and 4-hour working days o/a train strikes, you're lucky I've had long enough at my terminal to write to you.

Yours
George

2004 – Fighting fatigue

At another of the working lives seminars, Steve McGregor, Aston Villa's stamina consultant, spoke about fighting fatigue. The best way is to give up the 24/7 life of a central banker and become a professional footballer. All they have to do is run around a field for 90 minutes every Saturday during the winter. No wonder they don't get tired.

Origins of Flyleaf

Letter from Sir George Blunden

31st October 2003

Dear Paul,

Thanks very much for 'The Old Lady at Play'. I had quite forgotten about the bar profits. But it is nice to know that I once made a very fair and just decision. I'm sure anyone who paid for a drink at the Club would have preferred that the benefits should go to the Club rather than to the Bank. Probably it was the best decision I ever made in my 43 years at the Bank. Not that anyone ever made many decisions there!

My father started *Flyleaf* with Leslie Bonnet at the beginning of the thirties and kept co-writing it till his retirement in 1955. So I was particularly pleased to see two quotes from his time of involvement with it.

Sad about Basil Hone. But Denahy does some good work. My wife was delighted with the answer to how many people work in the Bank*.

Once again, many thanks
Yours ever
George

*One-third.

184

The Management Tree

as seen by Flyleaf

1. Made entirely of wood. Parts of it can be dead for years before they drop off
2. When a branch falls, most of the parasites which inhabited it, move back to the main structure
3. A large one can absorb hundreds of gallons of liquids each day
4. If not pruned regularly, it will not bear much fruit
5. Provides shelter for those underneath, but blocks out most of the light
6. Parts of it may be lit up for weeks at a time at Christmas
7. Monkeys can reach the top with remarkable speed
8. A person falling from the top can often grab a lower branch
9. A person falling from a lower level goes straight to the ground
10. Sometimes you can move from tree to tree without touching the ground, often travelling for considerable distances to a point at which you have absolutely no knowledge of the ground below

1935 – The Annual Arts and Crafts Society Exhibition
The ceiling of the Drapers' Hall was well worth seeing.

1945 – Overheard
'What am I doing today with enjoyment and self-approval which, in ten years' time, will make me squirm to think about it?'

1955 – Shorts from Reports
'Takes half the afternoon to explain that he is so busy that he hasn't time to do what you ask'

1965 – Letter to the Governor
Dear Sir,

You may or may not recall that my great grandfather, who was a servant of the Bank from 1852 – 1892, was required by the Drawing Office in the month of June 1874 to investigate a difference of threepence on the Private Accounts Section. These investigations, which lasted some four or five weeks, involved him in a certain amount of late work for which, under the rules applying at the time, he was entitled to twenty-one tea-tickets. Owing to an oversight on the part of the Staff section these tickets were never issued and I have calculated that the compound interest accruing on them now amounts to some £55,000 (or US$153,769) which sum I should be glad if you would forward to me at your earliest convenience.

Yours etc.,

Wilbur C Fish

JACKSON, OHIO

1975 – Christmas Luncheon
The luncheon will be served on all floors and no alternative menus will be offered on that day
Bank of England Club Notice dated 9th December 1974
The Editor reprinted it in Flyleaf under the heading
BUT ARE THEY CLEAN ENOUGH TO EAT OFF?

1985 – Short from report
Keeps subordinates very much on their toes – if only to prevent his dropped bricks landing on them

1995 – Dear Worried from Woking
Your problem was too specialised for me, so I rang the water company. They said that in a day or two they will have to turn off everybody's water because of the drought. When that happens take your thumb off the leaking pipe and go and ring a plumber.

2005 – Missing you already
The Health and Safety Executive has said:

'When you are off sick, returning to work as soon as possible may help you to get well'.

The Bank will set aside one of its turnstiles for staff who have highly contagious diseases. There will be another one for staff with five diseases or less and the rest of us can wheeze and stumble in through any of the others in the normal way.

* * * *

Flyleaf – A last look round
It is wise to forego an immediate advantage today. In order to gain a more lasting one tomorrow – provided, of course, that one is not so foolish as to die in the night.

Flyleaf – Forever England
UK Exchange Control Notice, 1955:
For ENGLAND read SCHEDULED TERRITORIES –

Nelson: The Scheduled Territories expect every man to do his duty

Brooke: If I should die think only this of me,
That there's some corner of a foreign field
That is for ever a Scheduled Territory

Flyleaf – 'Nations shall speak'
The motto of the BBC, *Nations Shall Speak Unto Nations* is quoted each week on the title page of the Radio Times. Surely it was a little tactless, however, to print immediately under it, in a recent issue, *'a battleship with its guns ready for action'*.

CHAPTER THIRTEEN

The Threadneedle Club

The Forty-Year Career

Every morning wet or fine
Enter all the clerks at nine
Like prison doors the lift gate crashes
Forty years to dust and ashes ...

Observe, O Lord, our shirts are clean
And help us catch the four-fifteen.
We order bitter by the half
and read the Daily Telegraph.

When our labours here are ended
Our little strength will be expended.
Take then, we pray, beneath Thy aegis
Our bungalows at Bognor Regis.

L F B Vale, Threadneedle Intercession, 1967

The Threadneedle Club

The Threadneedle Club, founded in 1985, is open to anyone who has worked in the Bank of England. At the end of 2007 there were 600 members.

In June 2008, the Club launched its new annual magazine, the *Threadneedle*, designed as a successor to *The Old Lady of Threadneedle Street*.

An annual list of members gives a contact number, current employment and dates of Bank of England service.

All good things come, sooner or later, to an end. Even in employment in the Bank of England. So, at some point, the decision will be taken – for whatever reason and after, say, five, ten, twenty or thirty years' service in the Bank – to move on to something new.

There will almost certainly be new opportunities and new horizons and almost all Bank leavers these days find new positions to their liking without difficulty or undue delay. But there will also be a need to build on the training and experience acquired in the Bank and a need for some channel to provide a thread of continuity between the old and the new.

It may also be very helpful to keep in contact – not only with good friends and close colleagues in the Bank but also a wider circle of acquaintance, as well as to have regular sight of the current Bank management and to have some understanding of current issues facing the Bank.

As time goes by, this contact often weakens and sometimes vanishes, just when it might be of most use. In today's employment climate, the majority of Bank leavers will have a three- or five-year contract from the new employer. At the end of the contract, if it is not renewed, there will be a further process of job application, evaluation on both sides and selection where again the period of service in the Bank will be taken into account.

What can be done at this later stage to reinforce this valuable network of contact and previous experience in the Bank?

Format of Events and Background

For the Annual Dinners, we agreed from the outset in 1985 to invite a Governor or Director, current or ex, as principal speaker, with other invitations to current and past members of staff who are generally asked to say a few words. This has proved a happy formula for badinage and Bank anecdotes, but has also provided valuable and seriously argued review of broader issues facing the Bank and the UK economy.

Annual Dinner – Lead Guests of Honour

1.	1986	Lord Richardson	Governor	1973–83
2.	1987	Lord O'Brien	Governor	1966–73
3.	1988	Sir Hector Laing	Director	1973–91
4.	1989	Sir Adrian Cadbury	Director	1970–94
5.	1990	Rodney Galpin	Director	1984–88
6.	1991	Sir George Blunden	Deputy Governor	1986–90
7.	1992	Lord Kingsdown	Governor	1983–93
8.	1993	Sir Jeremy Morse	Director 1965–72 & 93–97	
9.	1994	Lord George	Governor	1993–03
10.	1995	Sit Kit McMahon	Deputy Governor	1980–85
11.	1996	Brian Quinn	Director	1988–96
12.	1997	Tony Coleby	Director	1990–94
13.	1998	Lord George	Governor	1993–03
14.	1999	Ian Plenderleith	Director	1994–02
15.	2000	Michael Foot	Director	1996–98
16.	2001	Malcolm Gill	Chief Cashier	1988–91
17.	2002	Mervyn King	Governor	since 2003
18.	2003	Pen Kent	Director	1994–97
19.	2004	Lord George	Governor	1993–03
20.	2005	Howard Davies	Deputy Governor	1995–97
21.	2006	Rt Hon Lord Lawson of Blaby	Chancellor of the Exchequer	1983–89

Second Speaker
Admiral Jeremy de Halpert,   Deputy Master,
                                     Trinity House   since 2002

22. 2007 **Andrew Bailey**   Chief Cashier/
                                     Director   since 2003

Second Speaker
Garth Hewitt   Editor,
                                     The Old Lady   1996–2007

Chairman: Paul Tempest; Secretary: Gavin Gordon

Arrangements for 2008
Luncheon in Windsor Castle 18 July, 2008
Dinner in Trinity House, London, 20 October, 2008

CHAPTER FOURTEEN

From the Archives:

The Manila Bill of 1763

The Manila Surprise

Ye brave British Sailors, true sons of the Main,
Who scorn to submit to the insults of Spain,
Leave to Landmen their politic Schemes and their Talk
And enter on board the Lord Anson and Hawke.

The Wages, the Ingots, the Wealth of Peru,
The Spaniards are getting and boarding for you.
You shall ride in your Coaches, while Cowards shall walk
Who durst not engage in the Anson and Hawke.

Then aboard, my brave lads, and with Hearts stout and true
The Road unto Riches and Glory pursue
That your Wives may dress fine and your Children may talk
Of your noble exploits in the Anson and Hawke.

From a late 18th century recruiting poster

Lord Anson, over a period of 18 years, masterminded the expedition to Manila in 1762, but, dying suddenly in mid-summer 1762, never heard of the success of his Surprise.

Lord Hawke had planned and was present at the capture of Havana on 11–14 August 1762.

From the Archives
The Manila Bill of 1763

*T*he Bank of England, with ample vaults beneath its feet, has through decades and centuries been reluctant to throw anything away. Almost by default, it has preserved not only the bare bones of its three-century history but much of the day-to-day detail as well. For those historians who can gain access, here is a vast treasure-trove waiting to be explored. This is just one of hundreds of prime records, where lies a surprising story that is barely known.

I was first alerted to the Manila Bill in 1965 when I saw references to it in copies of The Old Lady *published in the mid-nineteen-thirties. It took me another twenty years to complete a feature article of my own on the subject which was published in* The Old Lady *in 1985. As was the tradition instigated by the Governor (later Lord) Norman in 1921 ('The OL is my passport to the world'), the magazine was distributed each quarter to friendly central banks all over the world. In due course, my article reached the Central Bank of the Philippines who remonstrated promptly at my reference to the troops opposing the British landings as 'several thousand wild local tribesmen'. 'They were', said another indignant letter of complaint, 'most probably far more civilised than the motley band of criminals, prisoners, deserters and ruffians that the British had brought with them.' Nonetheless, I was invited to Manila, first-class and a suite at the Manila Hotel, to talk about what I had found.*

By this time, in addition to all the relevant papers in the Bank, I had discovered from the National Maritime Museum data-base that they held, in locked trunks in their stores in Kidbrooke and Woolwich Dockyard, the ship's logs and associated papers of eight of the fourteen ships which had sailed to Manila in 1762. It took the Museum four months to find them and deliver them for my inspection in the Museum's

James Caird Library in Greenwich. Here, hour by hour, was simultaneous corroboration of what was in the official papers in the Public Record Office, the archives of the East India Company and the Bank of England.

In Manila, I realised that there were no prime records at all of the British occupation. The Spanish records, in 19 volumes were intact but had been transferred long ago to a Jesuit seminary in North-East Spain.

The Manila Bill is in the standard form of a London trade bill of exchange of its day. It is dated 18th February 1763 and is for 2 million Spanish dollars. The English version has a signed Spanish translation attached to it.

Both are signed by the Archbishop of Manila and drawn on the First Treasurer of his Catholic Majesty in Madrid. They are payable to Samuel Cornish, commander of the expedition and Vice-Admiral of the White.

What was really going on here? How did the Bank of England become involved? And why did the Manila Bill become such an embarrassment over a long period of time not only to the Spanish Government in its relations with the Philippines but also to both the British Government and the Bank of England?

The Manila Surprise

An 18th Century 'Pearl Harbour'

*T*he capitulation of Manila to the British at 18.00 on 6 October 1762 was a remarkable joint military and naval achievement. It was the first example of the practice of war on a global scale - the first extension of European power politics into the Pacific by the deliberate specific mobilisation and deployment of a substantial British military and naval invasion force sailing East from Madras and a strong Spanish garrison supplied and armed by galleon from Acapulco, Mexico. In this first 'round the world' world-war, the balance of power in the Western Pacific shifted as markedly and unexpectedly as in 1898-1900 and 1942-44.

In April 1764, following the end of the Seven Year War, the British garrison was withdrawn from Manila and the Spanish subsequently made every effort to erase this defeat and challenge to their power and influence from every account of their own presence in the Philippines. In England also, the event is hardly known today, having been eclipsed by the concurrent British capture of Havana and key French and Spanish colonies in the Caribbean as well as by a string of vital sea-battles and other invasions in the Atlantic and Mediterranean..

A Key Point in Philippine History

The 332-year occupation of the City of Manila and later the rest of the Philippines by the Spanish from 1565 to 1898, was followed by the occupation by the US military and US-led administration from 1899 until 1942 and the Japanese invasion and occupation from 1942 to 1945. The only respite came while the British were there in 1762-4.

From a letter from Admiral Cornish to the Bank of England

To the Governor and Court of Directors of the Bank of England, London

Manila The 2nd of March 1763

Gentlemen,

As the Money Concerns of Individuals is always considered most secure when under your Directions and Management, I have taken the Liberty in Behalf of myself and others entitled, to share in the Capture of Manila to remit to you the first of a sett of Bills of Exchange drawn by His Excellency Don Manuel Antonio, Archbishop of Manila, late Captain General and Governor of the Philippine Islands on his Catholick Majesty's High Treasurer at Madrid for the sum of Two Million of Spanish Dollars payable to my order in Consequence of the Terms of Capitulation signed by myself and Brigadier General Draper, the Archbishop and Ovidores* of the City of Manila...

I am Gentlemen

Your most obedient Humble Servant

Cornish

The Ovidores were the Manila City leaders who, with the Archbishop, were held captive in the Citadel pending full payment of the ransom bill

Transcribed from the original letter held in the Archive of the Bank of England, London, UK with the specific permission of the Governors of the Bank.

So in Manila, Cavite, Corregidor and in other cities, towns and villages, you find on the official monuments and national shrines today, first the name of Lapu-Lapu who drove the Spanish off in 1521, killing their commander, Ferdinand Magellan. Second come the Philippino patriots of 1762-4, who sided with the British. Some are designated 'national martyrs', as the Spanish hunted down and killed many of these rebels including the remarkable Maria Josefa Gabriela Silang, who had a hand in drafting the first Philippine Constitution. She was executed with her companions at Viga on 20 September 1763 .

So in the Philippines today, everyone knows that in 1762-64 the British supported the patriots and their independence movement and that the patriots mobilised irregulars to protect the British in Manila from Spanish attacks. But they have been largely unaware of what the British were doing there and know almost nothing of the wealth of archive material which has been discovered intact.

An Undercover Assignment in Canton

In 1759, a certain Colonel William Draper took sick-leave from soldiering in India to visit the city of Canton, an opportunity, it appeared, for him to do some relaxed sight-seeing with an old naval friend and to have a welcome break from military routine.

There was a hidden agenda. Draper was determined to gather discreetly from the European merchants in the trading-houses on Concession Island everything that was known about the state of the Spanish in Manila – the pattern of their extensive trade with China, the frequency of their supply and trading links across the Pacific to Acapulco, the size of the Spanish garrison, the state of the Intramuros, the fortress area constructed in the late 16th Century, surrounded by three miles of massive rampart and hitherto regarded as impregnable. His detailed report and

From the log of HMS Elizabeth in Manila Bay

30 September 1762

Weighed and ran down to Manila and Anchored off the fort in 4 fathoms of water as did the Weymouth. When moored, began to fire on the Fort. They hit it.

2 October 1762

Strong gale and squally wind with a great sea. PM – Struck yards and topmast and made everything snuff and let go the 3rd bower so that we rode with 3 anchors on the head.

At daylight saw the Southsea Castle Store Ship ashore with her Foremast gone. The enemy fired several shots at our Batteries.

Transcribed from the original log of HMS Elizabeth in the James Caird Library archives of the National Maritime Museum, Greenwich, UK.

maps identified the location of the batteries and the probable state of the cannon and defences both at Manila and at Cavite, the extensive fortified Spanish dockyard located within Manila Bay.

Draper duly delivered his report and the Spanish and Chinese maps and sailing instructions for Manila Bay to the Lords Anson and Egremont at the Admiralty and Foreign Office in London. These valuable and most secret papers were disclosed only to the Prime Minister, and one or two trusted friends and officials. Without Draper's enterprise and discretion and without the total confidentiality with which the report was handled, the events which followed could most probably never have taken place.

An Ocean Race with Secret Orders

In January 1762, almost six years into what became known as the Seven Years War between France and Great Britain, Spain declared war on Great Britain. Within a month of this declaration, the British Government had ordered the despatch of Draper on a small and very fast vessel, the *Argo*, 28 guns, carrying secret sealed orders for the Commander of the East India Squadron, then based in Madras.

The *Argo* left Portsmouth in March on what was to be one of the greatest ocean races of all time: a desperate race against time. Standing well off the hostile French and Spanish coasts, avoiding contact with any enemy vessel and enjoying fair winds and good weather for most of the twelve thousand-mile passage round the Cape, she was sailed flat out day and night under as much sail as she could carry. Only on the Coromandel Coast did she have the usual problems of flat calm, mist and pestering by local natives in their outrigger fishing canoes and trading catamarans.

The *Argo* arrived in Madras at end-June. The envelope carrying the Admiralty seal, was delivered and opened immediately by Rear-Admiral Samuel Cornish in his day cabin on the flagship, *HMS Norfolk.*

The East India Squadron was to provision immediately, embark an army under the command of General Draper, with full stores for an extended campaign and to proceed with all speed to mount an assault on the city of Manila. The immediate aim was to remove all aspects of Spanish control of the city and dockyards; the long-term objective was to undermine and indeed begin to destroy the 200-year dominance of the Spanish in the Pacific.

This was some four years before The Frenchman de Bourgainville set out on his Tahiti exploration voyage and six years before James Cook left London on the first of his three great voyages of discovery in the Pacific.

'Embark with all Haste'

Standing today on the fortress of Fort St George at Madras (now renamed Chennai), it is not difficult to imagine the dilemma Cornish faced. The East India Squadron was urgently in need of refitting. It had had several years of more or less continuous active service driving the French out of India, supporting General Clive's army ashore and most recently helping to take over the French stronghold of Pondicherry in conditions of great heat and ferocious resistance. The prisons ashore were crammed with French and other prisoners and there were local turbulent uprisings still to be contained. The Squadron was lying at anchor offshore with no facilities of a port nor any hope of loading alongside. Often a heavy swell and steep breaking waves on the beach prevented or impeded the taking on and off of men and stores.

The season was already late with monsoon storm winds expected in mid-September. Manila Bay, while a safe well-protected anchorage, was known to be subject to typhoons, violent wind-gusts, water-spouts and earthquakes. On the route, the passage of the Malacca Strait controlled by the Dutch presented navigational as well as security problems compounded by much random piracy and Dutch fears that their lucrative trading rights might be seized by force. Indeed the East India Company in Madras had expressed strong interest in finding a pretext to switch the attack to the Dutch in the Malacca Strait in preference to taking much bigger risks on a full war footing in Manila. Beyond Malacca, the East Indies Squadron would be in unknown waters with few good charts and many offshore dangers. As in Havana in the same year, surprise was essential: the objective was to catch the strong Spanish garrison as unprepared as possible. Delay was therefore unthinkable.

As far as an army was concerned, all that was available at Madras was Colonel Draper's 79th Regiment of Foot, much depleted by the recent hostilities and campaigns in India, together with a rudimentary company of Royal Artillery and several units of local sepoys. That was all.

Draper and Cornish met on 6 July and set the deadline of 1 August for departure. The Squadron set to work immediately, stripping down eight ships-of the line (over 50 guns each), the *Argo* and two frigates of 20 guns. The store-ship, the Southsea Castle, with a further 20 siege cannon and mortars, made for a total firepower of 598 guns. The prisons were emptied and their inmates impressed immediately into the British Army or as East India Company sepoys. They were trained, drilled and embarked.

Cornish despatched in advance a very fast frigate, the *Seahorse*, 20 guns, which had led the successful attack up the St Lawrence to capture Quebec in August 1759. Her orders were to block the Eastern end of the Malacca Strait and later the entrance to Manila Bay off the island of Corregidor in the hope that news of the impending arrival of the fleet could be kept from the Spanish.

Within three weeks of receiving the instructions from the Admiralty, the expedition was ready. A fleet of fourteen vessels loaded with stores for an extended stay carried a total complement of some 2300 souls.

The first group of ships led by *HMS Elizabeth*, 64 guns, was already under way from Madras on 29 July and the main fleet led by the Admiral in *Norfolk* left, according to plan, on 1 August. The whole fleet arrived safely to anchor in the Malacca Straits on 19 August and proceeded over seven days to take on fresh stores, food and water as well as much additional equipment for the assault.

Saturday or Sunday? – A Dispute over Time

On arrival in Manila Bay on 20–22 September after almost a month at sea, the fleet anchored first off Cavite, the large fortified naval shipyard of the Spanish. Noting the heavy surf and the long high line of the Intramuros fortification, the commanders could see no evidence of any preparation in Cavite or Manila for their arrival. It was therefore quickly decided to move the entire expedition along the coast to anchor within earshot of the capital. Here they were mystified to hear the church bells of the city ringing out for Sunday services on a Saturday.

Both London and Madrid kept the same time and the same Christian calendar. The British were as meticulous navigators as the Spanish – neither was likely to have made a mistake. It was left to Admiral Cornish to explain that, in the absence of an international dateline, the Spanish arriving from Madrid westwards-about through Mexico and across the Pacific would be one day later than the British arriving from London eastwards-about via India.

A Complete Surprise

The Spanish had been taken completely by surprise. They were not even aware that Spain was at war with Great Britain. Or that this large, hostile fleet was heading in their direction.

The Manila garrison consisted of about 600 seasoned Spanish troops and, according to British estimates, local levies said to number some 10,000. The Spanish were well-armed, mobile with many horses and mules and well-protected by the formidable 6-8 metre high ramparts of the Intramuros. These, little changed today, stretch 3.1 miles round the city and were then equipped with batteries of canon at the bastions, well-designed gates and the usual system of moats and free-fire killing-grounds close to the walls.

Divine Intervention – a Weather Surprise

Barely had a bridgehead been established on the beach than there was an ugly turn in the weather. Thick dark clouds filled the sky. The wind began to blow very hard indeed. Several cutters were overturned in the surf with some loss of life and there was much damage to arms and stores. All connection was lost between the fleet at anchor and the troops who had already landed on an open beach without protection and who were being harassed. At this point, to the joy of the Spanish watching in large numbers from the ramparts, the main store-ship, the *Southsea Castle* parted her cable and was driven onto the beach, losing her foremast and rigging. The church bells of the city were pealed in gratitude for the delivery of the city from the invader and the Archbishop issued a Promulgation, announcing that an Angel of the Lord had intervened to protect the city.

Curiously, the loss of the *Southsea Castle* proved a significant turning point. As the tide receded, the wreck provided a safe shelter for the troops both from the sporadic attacks and from the torrential tropical rain which persisted for several hours. The stores were all salvaged. Most important, Cornish and Draper had been at a loss as to how to unload the siege cannon, necessary for any attack on the city walls given the limited carrying capacity of their ship's boats, the heavy swell in the anchorage and the ferocity of the surf. It became a simple matter to lift all the cannon and mortars on the *Southsea Castle* out onto hard sand and to drag them on coconut matting sledges to establish siege batteries about one mile away close to the nearest corner of the ramparts at the San Diego Bastion. The Spanish had also not had time to clear the many wooden buildings which stretched up to the outer wall of the fortress at this point and these provided valuable cover for the attacking force.

Establishing a Lingua Franca

Initial exchanges between the joint British commanders and the Archbishop of Manila, who was both the religious and secular head of the Spanish garrison, proved disappointing and terms for a capitulation could not be agreed. A reliable translator to and from Spanish appeared to be lacking on the British side and there was some difficulty in finding a competent English speaker on the Spanish side. Fortunately, General Draper had enjoyed a traditional British education, passing through Bristol Grammar School and Eton en route to a fellowship at King's College, Cambridge. The Archbishop had also been well educated within the Church. Much of the official correspondence conducted each day over the following few months and preserved today both in Spain and in the British official records lodged with the Public Records Office was therefore expressed without any difficulty at all in Church Latin.

A Textbook Assault and Retreat

General Draper was well aware that the fortress walls were in a poor state-of-repair with many of the cannon on rotting gun-carriages in the planned attack area. He was, after a fierce fight, able to occupy buildings and a ruined church giving cover right up to the city-wall and obscuring the view of the Spanish defenders. The garrison, he had been told, should have consisted of 2000 European soldiers, but was much depleted. However, it soon became apparent that many of the local people had no love of the Spanish and were ready to co-operate fully with the British. Also, it became clear that the Spanish had organised an orderly withdrawal across the river behind the citadel taking almost all their women and children, as well as all the horses and mules to carry large quantities of treasure and arms. It was therefore quite easy for the Spanish to establish a new capital and stronghold in the town of Bulacan, well outside the reach of the British.

After several days of pounding by three siege batteries, an adequate breach was opened up to give access to the city. Within the walls, there was hardly any resistance from the few remaining Spanish defenders and the Archbishop, trapped in his battered citadel, was obliged to sign a formal capitulation.

The Manila Ransom

Under the terms of the Capitulation, the Spanish prisoners were guaranteed their lives, liberty, preservation of property, adherence to their religion and administration of their domestic affairs in return for the payment of a ransom of 4 million Spanish dollars. The capitulation covered the surrender of Spanish troops throughout that vast archipelago, although, in practice, British control was never extended much beyond Manila and Cavite.

This assault had been achieved with the loss of 6 British officers, 21 European soldiers and 5 sepoys. By any standard of naval and military efficiency, this was a remarkable performance completed in extreme weather and very difficult conditions: a text-book model of how the Navy and Army could co-operate to maximum effect, standing firm in adversity, relying extensively on each other, and exploiting every opportunity to the full.

Collecting the ransom proved a troublesome business. Finally, the gold, silver and other jewels, Chinese porcelain, silks and other artefacts assembled were valued at about 2 million Spanish dollars. The Archbishop readily agreed to pay the balance, the other half of the ransom, out of the 'situado', the annual payment in Mexican silver due to be delivered from Acapulco to cover the costs of the garrison and to finance trade. Two vessels, the *Panther* and the *Argo*, were immediately sent to look for the in-coming 'situado'galleon, the *Philippina*, which was already overdue.

Signing the Manila Bill

As the weeks went by with no sign of the *Philippina*, Draper and Cornish became restive, correctly suspecting a plot and treachery by the Spanish. By then, the *Philippina* had been spotted and warned by the Spanish. She was diverted, hidden and stripped: all the silver being transported safely to the provisional Spanish capital.

The British became suspicious and impatient. The Archbishop was summoned and 'persuaded' to sign a standard London bill of exchange for 2 million Spanish dollars drawn by himself on the First Treasurer of His Catholic Majesty in Madrid and payable to Cornish. The *Philippina* and her entire cargo were pledged as collateral to the bill. This bill, dated 18 February 1763, was accompanied by a flowery letter from Cornish to the Governor and Court of Directors of the Bank of England requesting collection of the proceeds and a letter from the Archbishop to the King of Spain, dictated by Cornish, explaining that the bill would be binding in case the delivery of the effects brought by the ship *Philippina* should not be made, were packaged together and brought back to England immediately by Draper on the fastest vessel in the fleet, the *Seahorse*.

By the time Draper got home, many things had happened. The war was over. A formal Treaty of Peace between Britain and Spain had been signed in Paris on 10 February, eight days before the bill was drawn and signed in Manila.

Collecting the Bill

The bill was duly delivered to the Deputy Governor of the Bank of England, John Weyland who sent it on immediately to Lord Halifax, the Foreign Secretary with a polite request that it should be presented for payment in the normal manner and that:

> '*His Catholic Majesty may direct the Two Millions to be put on one or more English ships of War as may happen to touch at Cadiz*'

In his reply and rejection of the Bill, the King of Spain enclosed a Memorial to be handed by the Spanish Ambassador in London to the British Government. It was based on a number of sound banking principles:

- The Archbishop of Manila had no authority to draw on the Spanish Treasury. It was wrong for the two British commanders to assume otherwise.
- The bill was drawn payable to an individual, not a government. This was firm evidence that it was part of a secret understanding arrived at by a number of private individuals for personal gain.

- The bill was dated eight days after the signing of the Peace Treaty and was therefore *ultra vires*.
- The ransom had been agreed to prevent loss of life and destruction of property. Yet, despite the Capitulation, the British troops had gone on a 40-hour rampage of pillage, and arson.
- The bill had been drafted by the British commanders and had only been signed by the Archbishop under extreme duress.

So the letters, together with the Bill and various copies in English and Spanish remain in the Archives of the Bank of England. The Bill is still unpaid and in strict accounting terms remains among the Bank of England's Miscellaneous Assets, an outstanding claim on the Government of Spain.

Refuting the Spanish Allegations

Draper, now Lt General Sir William Draper KB, laid up the Manila battle honours with much pomp in his old college chapel in King's College, Cambridge, then settled down in Manila Hall on Clifton Down, Bristol to write his 43-page refutation of the Spanish allegations, beginning in characteristic style:

> *'It is a known and universal Rule of War amongst the most civilised Nations, that Places taken by Storm, without any Capitulation, are subject to all the Miseries that the Conquerors may choose to inflict.'*

As far as the Spanish were concerned, his constant attention had been:

> *'. . .to the Preservation of those ungrateful People, who have almost taught me to believe that Humanity and Compassion are Crimes.'*

Now, his main concern was the restiveness of the returning troops, all expecting to recover something from the prize-money and a share in the proceeds of the bill. He pleaded with Lord Halifax in eloquent tones:

'Many of them, my Lord, from the too usual and sanguine hopes of their Profession, have already anticipated their supposed Profits, and may live to repent their fatal Success in a Jail; unless the powerful Intercession of the Government will rescue them from impending Misery and Destruction'.

In 1767, recognising a Spanish specialist of some resource and unflinching in his views, the British Government posted Draper as Lieutenant-Governor of Minorca, newly recaptured from the Spanish - just about as near as they could get him to Spain at that time and well out of the reach and beyond the range of his disappointed soldiers in London and Bristol.

More Surprises in Manila

Meanwhile, since Draper's departure, much had been going on in Manila. The *Panther* and *the Argo*, detached to look for the *Philippina*, had not yet found the incoming silver galleon. But, just as Draper had been about to return home, they were able to capture a very large outward-bound treasure galleon, which, having left Manila before the British arrived, had been disabled in the Pacific en route to Acapulco and had had to return to effect repairs. This prize, the Ponderosa *Santissima Trinidad*, was noted on arrival in Plymouth to be, at 2000 tons, one of the largest and strongest vessels ever to be seen so far in British waters. This helped to strengthen the Admiralty in their resolve to build a new super-class of battleship, the 100-gun First Rates following the specifications of *HMS Victory*, laid down at Chatham

Dockyard in 1759 and Nelson's flagship at Trafalgar in 1805. Estimates of the value of the rich cargo of the *Santissima Trinidad* varied greatly but seem to have settled at about the 2 million dollar mark. So, in the end, the equivalent of the outstanding amount of the Manila Ransom had, unintentionally, been delivered by the Spanish to the British in full.

Tea for Governor Drake

Left in charge of Manila and the Archbishop, Governor Drake continued patiently to collect up everything of value in the abandoned Spanish houses and churches, sending regular consignments home in old packing chests marked TEA FOR GOVERNOR DRAKE. Finally, instructions arrived for him to release the Archbishop and he and the British garrison said good-bye to their many Philippino friends, invited the Spanish to a farewell dinner and, in April 1764, sailed peacefully away.

After his return, Samuel Cornish was knighted and promoted Admiral of the White. He left his vast East Indies and Manila fortune to a nephew, Samuel Pitchford, who, as Captain of *HMS America*, 60 guns, had fought with him at Manila and who, in his own turn, rose to be Admiral of the Red.

The Falklands and Elsewhere

In 1767, it was proposed in Parliament to give the Falkland Islands to Spain in return for full settlement of the Manila bill. Dr Samuel Johnson and others had campaigned vigorously in favour of handing back the Falklands to Spain for free, if necessary, on the grounds that the costs of retaining those remote islands would far outweigh any possible future benefits. The British Government was reluctant to intervene and the King of Spain let it be known that he thought it prudent to decline so generous a proposal.

By then there were many other calls for compensation submitted to Parliament and to the press by the Manila Surprise soldiers, marines and sailors. These and their families persisted with their claims through at least two generations. From time to time, other tasty colonial morsels were suggested to persuade successive Kings of Spain to change their mind, but without effect. The Bank of England, to its acute irritation, was blamed repeatedly for being unable to secure payment of the bill.

Editor's Note

In 1996, while staying with the British Ambassador in Manila and briefing various ministers, I met Senator Gloria Macapagal Arroyo and, over breakfast, told her the story of the Manila Surprise. She encouraged me to write a book about it and to prepare some imaginative material for use in schools and the media in the Philippines. In the following year, I returned to mount an exhibition in the British Embassy Residence and on the Royal Yacht, Britannia then en route from the 1997 handover ceremonies in Hong Kong.

In 2002 a commemorative visit was arranged very close to the location of the 1762 British Assault Headquarters outside the San Diego Bastion of the Intramuros. A ceremony was held in the Manila Hotel at 18.00 on Sunday, 6 October 2002, precisely 240 years after the signature of the Capitulation by the Archbishop of Manila. I handed over to Gloria, now President of the Philippines and to First Gentleman Mike copies of my book The Manila Surprise *and facsimiles of the Ransom Bill and other key documents prepared specially for the purpose by the Bank of England. An expanded version of the book with copies of all the documents is to be published in London and Manila to celebrate the 250th Anniversary on 6 October 2012.*

THREADNEEDLE

June 2008

GUARDING THE GUARDIANS

ISSUE No. 1

of the new
Bank of England Threadneedle Club magazine,
successor to
The Old Lady of Threadneedle Street (1921–2007)

CONCLUSIONS

Shrinkage, Access and
the Mediatory Role

Bank of England Nursery Rhymes

Ride a cock-horse all the way to the Bourse,
Dismounting to see *The Old Lady*, of course
Bursting with bullion, and crammed full of cash,
You won't get any, so dinna ye fash.

Sing a song of wrong posts,
A ledger full of blots,
Four and twenty scratches out –
Initials missing? Lots!

Old Mother Hubbard went to the cupboard
To give her poor Clerks a dole,
She'd a key in her pocket, but couldn't unlock it.
It was under dual control.

Little Jack Horner sat in 'the Corner'
Dreaming of golf and beer,
At five in surprise he opened his eyes
And said 'What am I doing here?'

Baa, Baa Bank Clerk, have you any pay?
Yes Sir, yes Sir, so people say
Some of it the wife takes, taxes take the rest
And not a blooming cent is left to buy myself a vest.

Fortunello, The Old Lady, June 1922

Shrinkage, Access and the Mediatory Role

*M*any of the most venerable British institutions that have survived and prospered for centuries have only done so by intuitive serendipity and dexterity in the face of persistent political crisis or changing economic circumstances. Even the Royal Navy and many an infantry regiment has gone through difficult times. A resilient *esprit de corps* is essential to generate a determination to survive. The Bank of England is no exception. After 314 years, which way might 'The Old Lady of Threadneedle Street' be now heading?

Not Well Understood

Today, the Bank of England is not as well understood as it could be outside its own high, blank, protective walls. Until quite recently, the City of London's own 'Kremlin' has remained aloof and remote. The walls, constructed by Sir John Soane in 1795-1828, still present a formidable barrier, both physical and psychological, to communication and understanding. This may not have mattered much in the past, but it certainly matters today. Globalised financial markets and a public conditioned to expect transparency and backed by the media's constant demand for rights of access make the people suspicious of unnecessary secrecy. They expect minute-to-minute answers and seek a clearer grasp of what a central bank is doing and how it is likely to respond in any circumstance. The public image of the Bank as a sealed fortress locked in its past, has to be dismantled.

Some pessimists within the UK political arena predict that, sooner or later, the Bank of England will slip further into the clutches of the Government as many of its key functions are absorbed into the European Central Bank (ECB) in Frankfurt. The next steps would include the adoption of the Euro in the UK to replace the £sterling and the transfer of the Bank's interest-rate setting mechanism, the Monetary Policy Committee (MPC), to the ECB. What would remain of the Bank would be its function as local agent of the ECB under the direct control of the Treasury. From there on, the remaining central banking tasks and functions could be progressively outsourced by competitive tender.

Critical Mass

There is already a real danger ahead if the rundown of Bank staff continues. The numbers, approaching 7,000 when I was selected 50 years ago, were, at end-2007 1,555, 5 per cent less than a year earlier. This must be close to the critical mass needed for recruitment and career motivation. Why should the liveliest new graduates consider the Bank if they see only temporary employment and declining opportunity ahead?

No longer is it a matter of new recruits expecting to serve out their 40-year 'womb-to-tomb' careers in a variety of interesting jobs punctuated with outside assignments at home or abroad. There are no longer the additional-to-salary attractions of the past. In line with other leading banks, the 100 per cent housing loan at 2 per cent pa has long since vanished and the two-thirds non-contributory pension based on final salary has been whittled down. The Sports Club has been part-commercialised; the Bank yacht has been sold and not replaced; *The Old Lady of Threadneedle Street* quarterly magazine finally closed at end-2007 after 87 years. All this was inevitable and necessary. The decisions caused no surprise and fit the pattern and new style of the employment market today.

Today, people come and go, identifying themselves as itinerant professionals – economists, accountants, IT specialists, for example. Many arrive for a year or two in order to add the illustrious name of the Bank to their CVs and then leave, hoping to leap-frog their way up the public sector salary scales and career ladders. Or they storm off into the City hoping to make their fortunes as fast as they can. Team-building is seen less as a way of life, and more as a temporary and necessary network survival technique in the competitive jungle.

Increased transparency in a rapidly-evolving organisation demands a changing degree of accountability to the public it is serving. Where there was once scope for discreet market intervention or moral suasion, there is now less room to hide, a new illumination of hitherto dark and dusty places, a stripping away of the mystique and mystery. Yet no one wants the Grand Empress Britannia of Threadneedle Street, as in her logo enthroned on her own heap of gold, to end up as a frail old lady, shivering and ill-clad under the bright lights, clutching little more than a handful of worthless plastic and some out-of-date paper.

A turning point has, however, been reached and the measures taken have every chance of prolonging the good health of the Old Lady for many years to come.

UK Financial Services – A Vital Asset

Some understanding of the state of the City of London today is needed before we can get much further. Continuing expansion of international business in the City and the UK financial sector cannot be taken for granted. This already contributes over 6 per cent to UK Gross National Product and employs well over a million people. In global terms, the UK is No1 in international bond trading, foreign equities trading, foreign exchange trading and cross-border lending. In the UK banking sector, around half the assets are held by foreign banks and two-thirds of the 450 authorised banks are from abroad, nearly twice as many as in Frankfurt or New York.

Within the UK, the City has, of late, not always had a good press. High profits by the leading banks, a takeover feeding frenzy and million-dollar bonuses for directors, managers, dealers and lawyers, a spate of redundancies and short-time working have attracted public attention. The collapse of Northern Rock in 2007 highlighted weaknesses in the system. And the consequent outcry of customers, shareholders and other stakeholders has rubbed off on the Bank of England as the acknowledged 'lender of last resort' and guardian and guarantor of good behaviour in the financial sector.

Here the hiving off of the task of bank and financial sector supervision to the Financial Services Authority (FSA) in 1997 has blurred the issue. Already the FSA staff level is much higher than that in the Bank of England. Should the Bank of England resume its historical role as supervisor and decision-maker? Is such a rapidly expanding government institution as the FSA the best way to organise these things for the future? The public is confused and the wisdom of deepening the   division of responsibility in this area is questioned.

Contrary to   impressions among parts of the UK population, that the City is running into trouble, there is evidence that much of City international business is still buoyant, and that it is built on sure and strong foundations. So the City, for all its own recent bad press, has a tricky challenge of preserving and enhancing its own independence and prosperity in the years ahead while, at the same time, presenting an open and friendly public face and recognising the legitimate objectives and concerns of government. The Corporation and City of London has achieved much in this area and could do much more.

We have to pause to ask why the City has been so successful. Part of the answer in the banking sector is to be found not in London, but in New York, Tokyo and Frankfurt. First the US banks, then the Japanese and finally the German and French banks found that the benefits of channelling a significant part of their international business through their expanding branches in London far outweighed the disadvantages of distance and adaptation to a foreign culture. Access to the largest, most inter-co-ordinated and most vibrant financial market in the world was essential. In London these and many other foreign banks (364 in 2007) have found a genuine welcome. Their staffs have re-settled with minimum fuss and few formalities. Their London business has grown and blossomed, fully justifying the original decisions. Latterly, however, we seem to have reached another tipping point – some of the Japanese and other foreign banks have prudently decided that the latest fiscal and other costs of a London presence now outweigh the benefits and have voted with their feet.

A Long and Distinguished History

Among the leading global financial centres, London is unique as a centre where international issues dominate. The reputation of New York – and also Tokyo, Frankfurt, Paris rests primarily on the services they provide for their own national economies. None of these centres has a dedicated municipal authority to match the Corporation of London, older than the British Parliament, which focuses on providing and updating the infrastructure and international outreach that the London markets need to thrive. As a counterpart, the Bank of England has provided over a period of centuries – and continues to provide – the leading role model for other central banks and a safety-valve for the effective mobilisation of international finance.

The UK regulatory regime has generally been seen as straightforward, firm and fair. Today, banks, security houses, insurance companies and the markets in which they operate are regulated in such a way that problem resolution covering several disparate parts of the market, can be arranged promptly and conducted face-to-face. The main hope of the market is that these close relationships and effective self-regulation can be developed without imposing a heavy burden of costs or the tyranny of an inflexible and clumsy bureaucracy prone to political manipulation or immobilised by inertia.

Sterling is a hard currency used worldwide for centuries and well understood. Communications are conducted largely in English, the foremost world language for business and British commercial law is widely accepted worldwide for negotiating contracts and arranging arbitration. There are few barriers, apart from the control of money-laundering and other criminal activities, to the repatriation of profits and the rules governing the transfer of foreign-held assets are widely understood and respected.

A Challenge to the Bank's Reputation

For a period of several years, the Governors, Directors and several individual members of staff were placed under considerable strain. As explained in the Preface to this book, the Bank of England never flinched in its resistance to these allegations until good sense prevailed and the Bank was fully exonerated.

The Monetary Policy Committee – A Great Success

In one vital aspect, the Bank has enjoyed a major triumph over the last decade. In May 2007 the Bank celebrated the tenth anniversary of the Monetary Policy Committee

(MPC) which sets interest rates in the UK to achieve an agreed (and low) rate of inflation. Its consistent performance in achieving its target and thus controlling inflation and in intervening whenever it thinks that the economy is overheating or under-performing has earned wide respect. The process is more or less transparent and the MPC decisions, voting and reasoning are available for scrutiny by the press and open for discussion by the general public. The government has been released from a troublesome burden.

The markets consider the MPC as a strong new pillar of economic and financial stability and the broad weight of public opinion is enthusiastic. Despite the much stronger inflationary pressures now evident, they applaud the Bank's consistency of success in meeting the inflation targets and the significantly increased reliability of the Bank's economic predictions. For the time being at least, the Bank is in very good hands and its strength rests on the team which it has built to evaluate a much wider and more useful range of data.

The Role of the Governor

The general consensus today, based mainly on the outstanding success of the Monetary Policy Committee, is that the Bank of England has been soundly and wisely managed through a succession of crises and that, for the time being at least, it is in very good hands.

A Major Change of Direction within the UK

Over the last ten years there has been another major shift in the Bank's role within the national economy. From its foundation in 1694, the Bank of England was seen as a key intermediary between the British Government and the commercial interests of the City of London. Elements of this relationship remain, but they are not central to the fundamental purpose of the Bank of England today. While keeping close, the Bank no longer formally represents the City of London in its dealings with Government. The City is now well-equipped to perform this function itself. Rather, the Bank has recognised that with the new independent role of the MPC, it has to engage the entire UK population. Monetary and financial stability and the control of inflation (now begining to rise) affect everyone in the UK and repeatedly, the Bank emphasises that it is acting on behalf of the whole population, not merely a narrow business sector. Twelve full-time regional agents (*see* Annex 5), covering the entire area of the UK have been appointed. They and their staff are there to provide continuing contact with local business and industry, but also to consult and assess public opinion and expectations.

New Cooperation with Central Banks Elsewhere
Over the last five years, the new Centre for Central Banking Studies (CCBS) in the Bank of England has developed rapidly. Its 2007 programme of events involved more than 1,500 participants from 137 central banks round the world, following a flattening of interest in the leading US and international agency institutions specialising in this area. The aim of the CCBS is to define and promote best central banking practice across the whole range of global central banking, a listening as much as an educational role (see Annex 4). There is a strongly growing demand worldwide for CCBS training courses and professional consultations with China, France, India, Poland, Russia and Turkey at the head of the list. As far as the developing countries are concerned, the lead has been given by Argentina, Indonesia, Malaysia, Mexico, Pakistan, Philippines, Thailand, Uganda and Zambia.

A Rocky Ride Ahead

Within the next five to ten years, there are bound to be new political changes and economic crises to shake the UK economy as it moves back into rising dependence on imported energy and a further erosion of domestic manufacturing capacity. The financial sector will need to demonstrate its own ability to survive major shocks and to maintain or enhance its share of UK Gross National Product. For this to be fully understood by the public at large, both within the UK and elsewhere, will need, in addition to sound advice, prudent decision-making and effective action, a strengthened means of conveying the key issues – signals, icons, imaginative signposts. Where better to start than in the very heart of the City in the Bank of England?

What is required is a means of conveying imaginatively both the importance of the UK economy to its population country-wide and the global role of the UK financial sector, the opportunities it offers for enhancing and smoothing global economic growth, together with the potential it has for helping to resolve some of the dominant problems and uncertainties of poverty, health, food and energy supply and climate change.

A Footnote

As the Bank staff has shrunk within a very large building, it has not been possible, for security reasons to let it to commercial tenants. One option might be to expand the excellent Bank of England Museum currently reached from the East side of the Bank and to link it to the banking halls behind the Threadneedle Street façade. This major extension might be used in a variety of ways, say, for a public information centre covering global finance and/or the regional and national economy of the UK or to project

the global role of the City of London, using the latest
state-of-the-art technology to convey its message.
Throwing open the main entrance and this area to the
public might also have another psychological impact:
tangible evidence of the Bank of England opening up to the
public in general.

The Heart of the Matter

In this short book, I have tried to capture something of the
lively spirit of the old and present Bank of England. Not all
of it was good: there was drudgery in the multitude of
routine tasks and much frustration in the rigidity of the
career structure, most of which has now been eliminated.
The Bank of England today is a very different place from
what it was: it has shown ample evidence of an ability to
evolve and change to meet new circumstances. The Old
Lady still has a warm heart with patterns of sound public
service and close loyalties among its staff. There is, of
course, much less need and less time for the highly-
developed social, literary, musical and sporting life that
used to give a unique sparkle to a career in the Bank.

The most pressing priority is for the Bank of England to
continue to evolve. Just how the doors might be thrown
open in the quest for a new and open public face, a new
and friendly image for the new tasks ahead, rests essentially
with the Governors and Directors. The important thing is
that when the decision-makers and general public
worldwide think of the Bank of England, they have firmly
printed in their minds, much more than that of a fortress or
a museum image of the past, but also a firm impression of
continuity of purpose and a coherent, well-rounded, well-
argued vision of the future.

ANNEX 1

Governors of the Bank of England 1908 – 2008

1907 – 09	William Middleton Campbell
1909 – 11	Reginald Eden Johnston
1911 – 13	Alfred Clayton Cole
1913 – 18	Walter Cunliffe
1918 – 20	Brien Cokayne
1920 - 44	Montagu Collet Norman
1944 – 49	Thomas Sivewright Catto
1949 – 61	Cameron Fromanteel Cobbold
1961 – 66	Rowland Stanley (George) Baring
1966 – 73	Leslie Kenneth O'Brien
1973 – 83	Gordon William Humphreys Richardson
1983 – 93	Robert (Robin) Leigh-Pemberton
1993 – 2003	Edward Alan John George
2003 –	Mervyn Allister King

ANNEX 2

Members of the Court of the Bank of England at 1 March 2008

The Bank of England Act 1998, which came into force on 1 June 1998, changed the constitution and duties of the Court of Directors from that set out in the previous Act of 1946, strengthening the Bank's governance and accountability as well as formalising the Bank's responsibility for the conduct of monetary policy.

The 1998 Act provides for the appointment, by the Crown, of a Governor, two Deputy Governors and 16 Non-Executive Directors. The term of appointment for the Governor and Deputy Governors is five years and for the Directors, three years, all of which are renewable.

Court meets at least once a month, and its functions are to manage the Bank's affairs other than the formulation of monetary policy, which is the responsibility of the Monetary Policy Committee. This includes determining the Bank's objectives and strategy, ensuring the effective discharge of the Bank's functions and ensuring the most efficient use of the Bank's resources.

The members are:

Mervyn Allister King
Governor
from 1 July 2003 to 30 June 2013

Ms Rachel Lomax
Deputy Governor, Monetary Policy
from 1 July 2003 to 30 June 2008

Sir John Gieve, CB
Deputy Governor, Financial Stability
from 16 January 2006 to 15 January 2011

Brendan Paul Barber
General Secretary, Trades Union Congress
from 1 June 2003 to 31 May 2009

Roger Carr
Non-executive Chairman of Centrica plc
from 1 June 2007 to 31 May 2010

Ms Amelia Chilcott Fawcett, CBE
Chairman, Pensions First LLP
from 1 June 2004 to 31 May 2010

The Hon. Peter Jay
Former Economics Editor, BBC and previously
HM Ambassador to the USA
from 1 June 2003 to 31 May 2009

Professor Sir John Andrew Likierman
London Business School
from 1 June 2004 to 31 May 2010

Sir Callum McCarthy
Chairman, Financial Services Authority
from 22 September 2003 to 31 May 2008

Paul Myners
from 1 June 2005 to 31 May 2008

Sir Thomas John Parker
Chairman, National Grid plc
from 1 June 2004 to 31 May 2010

Ms Susan Rice, FCIBS, D.BA
Chief Executive, Lloyds TSB Scotland plc
from 1 June 2007 to 31 May 2010

Professor David William Rhind CBE, FRS, FBA
Vice Chancellor and Principal, the City University
from 1 June 2006 to 31 May 2009

Arun Sarin
Chief Executive, Vodafone Group plc.
from 1 June 2005 to 31 May 2008

James Murray Strachan
from 1 June 2006 to 31 May 2009

Robert Charles Michael Wigley
Chairman, EMEA, Merrill Lynch International
from 1 June 2006 to 31 May 2009

Geoffrey Charles George Wilkinson
from 1 March 2005 to 31 May 2008

Dr David Edwin Potter CBE
Chairman Psion plc
from 1 June 2003 to 31 May 2009

ANNEX 3

Members of the Bank of England Monetary Policy Committee at 1 March 2008

Interest rates are set by the Bank's Monetary Policy Committee. The MPC sets an interest rate it judges will enable the inflation target to be met. The Bank's Monetary Policy Committee is made up of nine members – the Governor, the two Deputy Governors, the Bank's Chief Economist, the Executive Director for Markets and four external members appointed directly by the Chancellor. The appointment of external members is designed to ensure that the MPC benefits from thinking and expertise in addition to that gained inside the Bank of England.

Members serve fixed terms, after which they may be replaced or re-appointed.

The members at 1 March 2008 were:

Mervyn King, Governor
Rachel Lomax, Deputy Governor
Sir John Gieve, Deputy Governor
Kate Barker
Charles Bean
Tim Besley
Prof. David Blanchflower
Andrew Sentance
Paul Tucker

Each member of the MPC has expertise in the field of economics and monetary policy. Members do not represent individual groups or areas. They are independent. Each member of the Committee has a vote to set interest rates at the level they believe is consistent with meeting the inflation target. The MPC's decision is made on the basis of one-person, one-vote. It is not based on a consensus of opinion. It reflects the votes of each individual member of the Committee.

A representative from the Treasury also sits with the Committee at its meetings.

ANNEX 4

The Centre for Central Banking Studies in the Bank of England Activities 2005–2007

	2005	2006	2007
London events			
Number of London events	28	28	27
Number of participants	600	589	608
International Events			
Number of International Events	27	24	37
Number of participants (in seminars/conferences)	691	548	916
Total Number of participants	1291	1137	1524

Seminars and Conferences in London in 2007 were titled: Inflation Targeting; Empirical Finance for Central Banks; Exchange Rates and Capital Flows; Financial Stability (3); Financial Regulation; Managing Surplus Liquidity; The Structure of Financial Markets Liquidity Forecasting; Central Bank and Government Securities Issuance; and Economic and Financial Modelling(4).

CCBS Seminars and Workshops were held overseas in 2007 in Armenia, Austria, Bulgaria, Chile; Costa Rica; Egypt; Hong Kong; South Korea; Latvia; Macedonia; Malaysia; Mexico; Montenegro; Pakistan; Poland; Samoa; Sierra Leone; Singapore;

South Africa; Tanzania; Thailand; Uganda; Ukraine; United Arab Emirates and Zambia. Also CCBS experts visited at the request of the relevant central banks Colombia, Libya, Lithuania; Malta; Mauritius; Palestine and Syria.

The text of all CCBS handbooks (33 at end-2007) can be downloaded worldwide from the CCBS website at *www.bankof england.co.uk/education/ccbs/handbooks_lectures.htm*. This listing also indicates which handbooks are available in Arabic, Russian and Spanish.

Seminars, Workshops and Forums arranged by CCBS in London for September-December 2008 include:

Operational Risk Management (workshop, 1-4 September); Financial Stability: an overview (8-12 September); Structure of financial markets (15-19 September); Liquidity Forecasting (22-26 September); Key Policy Issues for Central Banks (senior management seminar 6-8 October); Financial Risk Globalisation and Disintermediation – Implications for Central Banks (selected economists' research forum (14-17 October); Design, Development and Operation of Payment Systems (expert forum 21-23 October); Exchange Rates and Capital Flows (27-31 October); Practical Policy Analysis of Financial Regulation (3-7 November); General Equilibrium Models for Monetary Policy (10-14 November); Topical Issues in Human Resources (expert forum, 19-21 November); Financial Stability (expert forum, 25-27 November; Economic modelling and forecasting (1-12 December).

Senior Staff of the CCBS at end-2007: Mario I. Blejer (Director); Gill Hammond (Deputy Director) Celine Gondat-Larralde; Kevin James; Sue Milton; Mohamed Norat; Ole Rummel; Ibrahim Stevens; Francesco Zanetti.

ANNEX 5

The 12 Regional Agents of the Bank of England (as at 01.01.08)

South East and East Anglia	Chris Bailey
West Midlands	John Bartlett
East Midlands	Chris Brown
North East	David Buffham
South West	Kevin Butler
Northern Ireland	Phil Eckersley
Yorkshire and the Humber	Paul Fullerton
London	Wendy Hyde
Wales	Adrian Piper
Scotland	Tony Strachan
Central Southern England	John Whitley
North West	John Young

ACKNOWLEDGEMENTS

I would like first to pay tribute to the late Basil Hone. I first met him (alias in anagram Ben Shailo of *The Daily Telegraph*) in the Chief Cashier's Office in 1961, where, for three months, we shared the dubious distinction of managing the accounts of the Ruler of Kuwait. These vast holdings – the reserves of the state and surplus oil revenue in sterling – threatened to bring the UK economy to its knees, if Kuwait were ever to decide to switch them abruptly into dollars or Deutschmarks or yen. (Praise be to Allah, they never did). Basil would sit opposite me every morning, drawing furiously to meet his daily 11.00 am cartoon deadline, while I sorted out the work for the day. Thanks to him and Margot, we now have a collection of 300 *Old Lady* cartoons for this and the two follow-up volumes to come.

Second, Danny Denahy, who has illustrated *The Old Lady* brilliantly for over thirty years and who today can be relied upon to produce beautifully in full colour within a couple of days, anything I ask him for.

Third, Stacey International. To step through their doorway in Kensington Church Street is always like stepping into another world fizzing with wit and excitement. To Tom Stacey, Max Scott and the (now independent) designer Kitty Carruthers and the rest of their staff, I owe many thanks indeed.

Fourth, the members of The Threadneedle Club, of whom a dozen have contributed to this volume and the many other contributors of whom the earliest was writing in 1808 and the latest in 2008. The Threadneedle Club has been a valuable network of use both to its members and to the Bank of England itself, providing a well-spring of anecdote and memories.

Finally, my wife, Jennifer who, since 1961, has had to put up patiently with the other woman in my life, albeit a lady of maturity and courage, endowed with wit, compassion and an innate and irrepressible serendipity.

Paul Tempest
June 2008